Champion

Ishy Din

methuen | drama

LONDON • NEW YORK • OXFORD • NEW DELHI • SYDNEY

METHUEN DRAMA

Bloomsbury Publishing Plc, 50 Bedford Square, London, WC1B 3DP, UK
Bloomsbury Publishing Inc, 1385 Broadway, New York, NY 10018, USA
Bloomsbury Publishing Ireland, 29 Earlsfort Terrace, Dublin 2,
D02 AY28, Ireland

BLOOMSBURY, METHUEN DRAMA and the Methuen
Drama logo are trademarks of Bloomsbury Publishing Plc.

First published in Great Britain 2025

A catalogue record for this book is available from the British Library.

A catalog record for this book is available from the Library of Congress.

ISBN: PB: 978-1-3505-6635-4
ePDF: 978-1-3505-6637-8
eBook: 978-1-3505-6636-1

Series: Modern Plays

Typeset by Mark Heslington Ltd, Scarborough, North Yorkshire

For product safety related questions contact
productsafety@bloomsbury.com.

To find out more about our authors and books visit
www.bloomsbury.com and sign up for our newsletters.

A Live Theatre production

CHAMPION

By Ishy Din

CHAMPION

By **Ishy Din**

Thursday 13 February – Saturday 8 March 2025

Summer 1977. South Shields. Muhammad Ali is coming to town.

Set around the great boxer's now-legendary visit to the North East, this searing new drama shows the effect that such a major event has on a mixed-race family in South Shields.

Written by one of contemporary theatre's most regarded writers, this epic dramatic offering stirs up questions of identity, community and what each of us is fighting for.

Two brothers' lives are turned upside down in a punchy play that hits hard!

CAST

Christina Berriman Dawson	Sheila
Jack Robertson	Billy
Daniel Zareie	Azeem

CREATIVE & PRODUCTION TEAM

Ishy Din	Writer
Jack McNamara	Director
Amy Watts	Designer
Drummond Orr	Lighting Designer/Production Manager
Matthew Tuckey	Sound Designer
Lou Duffy	Costume
Alicia Meehan	Movement Director
Taylor Howie	Technician
Craig Davidson	Stage Manager
Chloe Ribbens	Deputy Stage Manager
JD Stewart	New Work Producer
John Dawson	Artist Development Producer
Von Fox Promotions	Photography
Tommy Chavennes	Trailer production

Muhammad Ali and Me by Ishy Din

I share a birthday with Muhammad Ali, 17 January. It's a fact I crowbar into any conversation about the great man. Admittedly, it's a tenuous link, in my humble opinion, to the greatest sportsman of all time. But I care not a jot. It fills me with pride, and I bask in the reflected glory of being born on the same day as him.

I was born in Middlesbrough, some 27 years after my idol. Our small town on the North-East coast relied on the steelworks for its main source of employment. Everybody had a father, brother or uncle who worked there. For me, childhood was innocent, although for my older siblings, it was different. Racist attacks were rife, and racist murders often made the headlines. Yet my earliest televisual memories are of *Nai Zindagi Naya Jeevan* – an Urdu-language programme – and Muhammad Ali's fights.

I could give or take *Nai Zindagi Naya Jeevan*. It was brown people speaking Urdu on TV, and though the rest of my family were avid viewers, as an eight-year-old, I was indifferent, although when I grew older I understood why it was so important to them. The Ali fights, however, are seared into my memory. They were events. We'd stay awake, my siblings and father discussing the bout with excitement and 'authority'. Predictions were made – not about if Ali would win, but how and when. Would it be a knockout or a stoppage?

At that tender age, I had no idea who Ali really was. I didn't grasp his achievements, his politics, or his pugilistic prowess. I was simply swept up in the collective excitement that engulfed our house. Before each fight, Ali would pray, raising his hands just as my devout Muslim mother did when finishing her obligatory prayers. He referenced Allah, as everyone in my tiny orbit did in some way. When someone said 'Ali', we all knew who they meant. Muhammad Ali seeped into my life before I even understood who he was.

As I grew older, my understanding deepened. The more I learned, the more I wanted to know. I devoured books, interviews, articles and TV appearances. Ali wasn't just a boxer; in the ring he was graceful, dynamic and powerful . . . he truly did *'float like a butterfly and sting like a bee'*. Outside of it, he was an activist, an entertainer, a poet and a revolutionary. He spoke of justice, equality and pride. He debated the brightest minds and left them floundering. As he famously told Parkinson, *'You can't beat me, mentally or physically.'*

For a young British Pakistani Muslim growing up in the North-East, Ali was the brightest star in the universe.

Yet later still, his flaws and complexity became apparent – but any compelling character needs to be flawed. It is this complexity, this imperfection, that resonates with us as a species, as fellow human beings.

In 1977, Ali came to South Shields, just up the road from Middlesbrough. The town, known for its maritime history, had its own working-class struggles and a small but vibrant Muslim community, made up mostly of Yemeni sailors and their descendants. They too were no strangers to racial conflict.

Johnny Walker, a painter and decorator who also ran a boxing club in South Shields, went to America to ask Ali, who was well known for supporting charitable causes, to come and help raise money for local boys' clubs. Much to the surprise of Tynesiders, Ali agreed. Not only did he agree he waived the cost of the trip, some £7,000, a huge amount in 1977, in order for that money to go towards the cause.

When Live Theatre; with a long and illustrious history of filling its deceptively small space with epic stories that resonate with a wider world, asked me to write a play for them, I couldn't think of a more fitting subject than Ali's visit.

But how to get under the skin of the story?

I decided to tell the story through a mixed-race, Irish-Pakistani family grappling with grief, identity and their place in the world. It felt reflective of where we are as a society now.

During my research I found that Ali's visit brought a rare sense of unity to South Shields. For one brief moment, barriers of race, religion and class dissolved. The people of South Shields, regardless of background, were united in admiration for Ali. He wasn't just a champion in the ring; he was a champion of humanity, using his platform to uplift others. In a region often overlooked, Ali's visit felt like validation to them – a reminder that even their small corner of the world mattered.

In a piece of serendipity for any writer, the King's visit coincided with that of The Queen, who was celebrating 25 years on the throne. She too came to South Shields (the day before), and walked amongst her subjects on Gypsies Green. I am reliably informed that the crowds were bigger for Ali.

For the Muslim community, his visit was transformative. It reaffirmed our cultural and spiritual identity at a time when representation was scarce. Ali's confidence in navigating his faith gave a blueprint for carrying oneself with pride. In a society where we often felt invisible, Ali made us feel seen.

Reflecting on his visit now, I feel that it has reiterated to me that our stories, no matter how local, can resonate universally. Ali's visit wasn't just a footnote in his life; it underscored the interconnectedness of people and places and showed how a global icon could touch lives in the most unexpected settings.

My play seeks to capture the essence of that visit – the anticipation, the joy, the significance. It's not just about Ali, but about South Shields – the people and a family that is profoundly affected by it. It's about a town's intersection with history and how that moment continues to ripple through time. In dramatising his visit, I hope to honour both Ali's legacy and the spirit of the community that embraced him.

For South Shields, Ali's visit remains a point of pride, a testament to the town's openness and resilience. For me, it's a touchstone, a reminder of the power of representation and storytelling. Ali's legacy as a boxer is unparalleled, but his legacy as a man who stood for justice, faith and humanity continues to inspire.

In a world where divisions often seem insurmountable, Ali's visit to South Shields is a poignant reminder of the connections that unite us. His presence was a gif – a moment of transcendence affirming our shared humanity. For a young Muslim boy in the North-East, it was a beacon of hope, proof that greatness could find its way even to the smallest of towns.

Cast

Christina Berriman Dawson – Sheila

Christina's theatre credits include: *RSC 37 Plays*, *Northern Stage*, *Pinocchio* (Theatre Royal, Newcastle); *The Odyssey* (National Theatre); *The Wasp* (Customs House); *Gaze* (Northern Stage); *Art of Facing Fear* (Theatre Os Satyros); *Credit* (Cap-a-Pie); *Sugar* (Open Clasp, BBC iPlayer); *Goldilocks & the Three Bears* (Theatre Royal, Newcastle); *Under Milk Wood* (Northern Stage); *Rattlesnake* (Open Clasp); *Beyond The End Of The Road* (November Club-Tour/SAGE); *Key Change* (New York Theatre workshop, Off Broadway and UK National Tour & Live filming Space/BBC); *Sugar* (Open Clasp at Live Theatre); *5 Dead Nobodies* (Customs House); *Clothes Swap Theatre Party* (Forward Theatre & Derby Playhouse); *Dolly Mixtures* (Customs House); *Make do and Mend*, *From there to you, from here to me* (Odd Man Out); *Turning Pages* (Live Theatre); *Season Ticket R&D* (Northern Stage); *The Frights* (Alphabetti Theatre & Theatre N16 London); *Hull's Angel* (Ensemble 52); *Gaslight On Grey Street* (Theatre Royal Studio); *Pied Piper Project & Cautionary Tales From The Trenches* (November Club); *Flock* (ZENDEH); *Dick Whittington*, *Aladdin* (Barnsley Lamp Room Theatre); *The Selkie* (Sage Gateshead); *The Bodies* (Live Theatre) and recently finished panto *The Little Mermaid* (Theatre Royal, Newcastle).

Other credits: *Nowt to Look At* (BBC Radio Drama); *George Gently* (BBC); *The Hunt for Raoul Moat* (ITV); feature film *The Magdalene Sisters*.

Jack Robertson – Billy

Jack wrote and starred in his own BBC short *Where It Ends*, which was nominated for a BAFTA. He starred in *Gerry & Sewell* at both Live Theatre and Theatre Royal Newcastle. He also created an ensemble sketch group *Metroland Comedy*, which was selected by *The Guardian* as a 'Top 10 Pick' to watch at the Fringe.

Other credits include: *Danny & Mick* (CBBC); *Inspector George Gently* (ITV); Will Oldroyd's *Lady Macbeth*.

Daniel Zareie – Azeem

Dani is currently training at Newcastle Theatre Royal's year-long actor training course Project A, during which he has performed in the critically acclaimed *Gerry and Sewell*. In addition to this, as part of Project A he has performed in Berkoff's *The Bow of Ulysses* as well as Dennis Kelly's *Orphans*. He also performed Northern Stage's *Am I Alone in This* as part of Northern Stage's Young Company. This is Dani's first professional contract.

Creative & Production Team

Ishy Din Writer

Ishy Din is a critically acclaimed playwright and screenwriter whose work spans stage, television, film and radio, often drawing on his unique experiences and cultural background.

Ishy is currently an Associate Playwright at the Royal Court. He is under commission to both the Royal Shakespeare Company and The Kiln Theatre in London. Ishy was a writer on *Silence*, a play about the partition of India for Tara Theatre and the Donmar Warehouse. His play *Approaching Empty*, a co-production between Tamasha, The Kiln and Live Theatre Newcastle, premiered at The Kiln Theatre in January 2019 before embarking on a national tour. In 2016, *Wipers*, a Leicester Curve/Watford Palace/Belgrade Theatre co-production, explored the untold stories of South Asian soldiers during the First World War and toured extensively. Ishy's monologue for Company TSU was featured in the double bill *Beats North*, which played at the Edinburgh Fringe Festival in 2014 and toured the UK. His breakthrough play *Snookered*, produced by Tamasha, Oldham Coliseum and The Bush Theatre, toured in 2012 and ran for four weeks at The Bush Theatre in London. The play won the Best New Play award at the Manchester Theatre Awards in 2013. Ishy also served as the 2012 Pearson Writer in Residence at the Manchester Royal Exchange.

Ishy's television credits include writing for *Phoenix Park* (CBBC), Sky's *Atomic Bazaar* (Pulse Films). Other notable credits include *Shakespeare & Hathaway* (BBC) and *Ackley Bridge* (The Forge/C4). In 2018, his live theatre broadcast *Taxi Tales*, produced by Tamasha, aired on BBC Two as part of the BBC Live project. Ishy participated in the BBC TV Drama Writers Programme (2016) and Media XChange's Advanced Writing for Television Drama Programme (2017). He also wrote *Life's Like That* for the BBC TV *Brief*

Encounters strand and *Doughnuts*, a standalone comedy-drama for Channel 4's *Coming Up* season in 2013.

His film work includes the short film *Our Lad*, directed by Rachna Suri, which was featured at international festivals, and *Perfume*, created for Eclipse Theatre's 10 x 10 online project.

Ishy's radio work includes *John Barnes Saved My Life* for BBC Radio 5 Live, *Whose Baby* for BBC Radio 4, and *Parking and Pakoras* for local radio.

Jack McNamara Director

Jack has been Artistic Director and Joint CEO of Live Theatre in Newcastle since 2021. Productions for the company as director include: *Saint Maud, The Bounds, The Cold Buffet, We Are The Best!, One Off.* Previously he was Artistic Director of New Perspectives in Nottingham, where productions included the multiple award-winning *The Fishermen* (West End, Home Manchester, BBC Radio 3, British Council Showcase); *The Lovesong of Alfred J. Hitchcock* (Off Broadway); *The Boss of it All* (Soho Theatre/Offie Nominated); *Darkness Darkness* (Nottingham Playhouse) and first national tours of plays by Athol Fugard and debbie tucker green, among many others. Recent freelance work includes *Shy* by Max Porter (Southbank Centre) starring Toby Jones and Ruth Wilson. He directed the epic audiobook *Voice of the Fire* by Alan Moore starring Maxine Peake, Mark Gatiss and Jason Williamson of Sleaford Mods.

Drummond Orr Lighting Designer/Production Manager

Drummond has over forty years' experience as a theatre electrician, technical manager, lighting designer and production manager. In that time, he has toured nationally and internationally. Lighting design credits include: *Motherland, Captain Amazing* (Live Theatre/Edinburgh

Fringe); *Cilla and Me, Iris, My Romantic History, Tyne, The Prize, Nativities, Harriet Martineau Dreams of Dancing, The Cold Buffet, Three Acts of Love, Saint Maud* (Live Theatre); *The Bounds* (Live Theatre/Royal Court); *The Red Lion* (Live Theatre/Trafalgar Studios); *Cooking With Elvis* (Live Theatre/Assembly Rooms); *Wet House* (Live Theatre/Hull Truck/Soho Theatre); *A Walk On Part* (LiveTheatre/Soho Theatre/Arts Theatre); *The Girl in the Yellow Dress* (Market Theatre, Johannesburg/Grahamstown Festival/Baxter Theatre, Cape Town/Citizens, Glasgow); *Educating Rita* (Theatre by the Lake/David Pugh and UK Tour).

Matthew Tuckey Sound Designer

Matthew is a Sound Designer and Sound Artist working across theatre, music, installation, podcast and film. He is also a board member for the Association for Sound Design and Production.

His recent work as Sound Designer includes: *Champion, Saint Maud* (Live Theatre); *The Bounds* (Live Theatre and The Royal Court); *Festen* (Royal Central School of Speech and Drama); *Love It If We Beat Them* (Live Theatre in association with Emmerson & Ward); *The Sorcerer's Apprentice* (Northern Stage); *Josey* R&D, *Repeat Signal, Lost Found and Told: New Tales for Northumberland* (November Club); *Wolf!* (Kitchen Zoo in association with Northern Stage); *joey* (gobscure in association with Greyscale Theatre); *Floorboards, Trolley Boy, Walter* (Alphabetti Theatre).

His work as Associate Sound Designer includes: *Macbeth* (English Touring Theatre and the Lyric Hammersmith Theatre); *Underdog: The Other Other Brontë* (Northern Stage and National Theare); *Under The Sea* (Tiny Dragon Productions); *You Heard Me* (Luca Rutherford); *A Christmas Carol* (Northern Stage); *Oh No, George!* (Can't Sit Still); *Stella* (Filskit Theatre).

His work as Sound Artist includes: *The Rime* (multi-channel immersive installation); *An Audio Diary in Binaural*, January 2021 (digital piece for headphones); *South Bend* (05–06/20) (digital EP); *Fed Up, Foodbank Histories Project* (digital piece for headphones for Newcastle University Oral History Unit & Collective).

Amy Watts Designer

Amy Watts is a recently-returned North-Eastern Set and Costume Designer. Graduating from Wimbledon College of Art with a BA (Hons) in Theatre Design, she has since worked for over a decade in the industry on a wide variety of different projects.

Designer: *Peter Pan and Wendy* (Durham Gala); *The Deep* and *Stones In His Pockets* (Eastern Angles); *Three Acts of Love, Good Timin* and *West End Girls* (Live Theatre); *Bat with No Bite* and *The Hound of the Baskervilles* (Northern Stage); *Much Ado About Nothing* (Creation Theatre); *Hedda Gabler* and *A Midsummer Night's Dream* (Reading Rep); *Rapunzel, Jack, Mum and the Beanstalk* and *Princess and the Frog* (Hull Truck); *The Massive Tragedy of Madame Bovary* (Jermyn Street Theatre); *The Unlocked Door* (Seaton Delaval Hall with 'The November Club'); *The Wasp* (Customs House); *The Hound of the Baskervilles* (East Riding Theatre); *The Remarkable Robin Armstrong's Extraordinary Christmas Adventure* (Hexham Theatre); *The Legend of Sleepy Hollow* (UK Tour); *Story Project Rage, Romance and Resolution, Miss Havisham's Wedding Night*, and *12 Poems of Emily Dickinson* (Arcola Theatre); *Grand Hotel, Lend me a Tenor, 9 to 5* and *King of Hearts* (London School of Musical Theatre).

About Live Theatre

'One of the most fertile crucibles of new writing' **The Guardian**

Our vision is for a North East that writes its own story and fights for a more creative future

Live Theatre occupies a unique place as one of the country's only dedicated new writing buildings outside of London. Across its fifty-one-year history it has launched the careers of many of today's leading theatre figures and continues to develop and platform the artists of tomorrow, from playwrights to local school children. Deeply connected to its region and unafraid to confront the most pressing issues of our time, Live Theatre brings ambitious regional artists and adventurous local audiences into vivid contact.

Our mission is to unearth the rich and unexpected narratives of our region, to nurture creativity and bring passionate ideas to life and to be a space that unites people and ignites imaginations.

'Live Theatre has supported generation after generation of new writers, actors and theatre artists.' **Lee Hall, Playwright**

To learn more about Live Theatre and get involved, see www.live.org.uk

Best Friends

Noreen Bates
Jim Beirne
Michael and Pat Brown
George Caulkin
Helen Coyne
Christine Elton
Chris Foy
Robson Green

Brenna Hobson
John and Liz Holmes
John Jordan
Graham Maddick
Elaine Orrick
Paul Shevlin
Margaret and John Shipley
Shelagh Stephenson

Sting
Alan Tailford
David Walton

Good Friends

Vincent Allen
John Appleton
Zoe Blakemore
Jeff Brown
Alec Collerton
Chris Connell and Lucy Nichol
Ron Cook
Lynda and Mike Dillon
Ross Freeman
Ann Gittins
Beverley Jewitt
Eileen Jones
John Mason

Friends

Pat Allcorn
Patricia Arnold
Marjorie Baillie
Norma Banfi
Simon Barker
Tanya Barker
Jill Barnes
Bex Bowsher
Lawrence Bryson
Rob Chapman
Sally-Anne Cooper
Angela Cooper
Judy Cowgill
Nigel Cross
Glynis Downie
Suky Drummond
Ross Elgie
Keith Elliott

Susan Wear
Sue Wilson
Lucy Winskell

Rhys McKinnell
Linda Norris
Michelle Percy
Pat Ritchie
Michelle Robinson
Martin Saunders
Phil Skingley
Susan and Mike Stewart
John Stokel-Walker
John Tomaney
Angela Walton
K F Walton
Mary and Steve Wootten

Sue Emmas
Robert Fairfax
Moira Gray
Norma Harris
Gael Henry
Ruth and Robert Heyman
Gillian Hitchenes
Wendy Holland
Irene Hudson
Nicole Kavanagh-Stubbs
Michael McBride
Rachael McCabe
Michele McCallion
Ian McPherson
Catherine Moody
Linda Moss
David Nellist
Michael Nielsen

Jean Ollerton
Mark Olney
Clare Overton
Janis Proudfoot
David Robertson
Jo Robinson
Julian Rogan
Jean Scott
Jill Scrimshaw
Alan and Rosalind Share
Monica Shaw
Jo Shepherd

Ian and Christine
Shepherdson
Tracey Sinclair
David Slater
Brent Taylorson
Don Tennet
Robert Vardill
Sandra Wake
Jennifer Wallace
Sue Ward
Ann Watts
Heather Wilkinson
Keith Williamson

Plus those who choose to remain anonymous

Live Theatre Staff

Executive Director/Joint Chief Executive
Jacqui Kell

Artistic Director/Joint Chief Executive
Jack McNamara

PA to Joint Chief Executives
Alex Readman

Creative Programme

New Work Producer
JD Stewart

Artist Development Producer
John Dawson

Associate Artists
gobscure
Kemi-Bo Jacobs

Children and Young People

CYPP Leader
Helen Green

Senior Creative Associate CYPP
Paul James

CYPP Administrator
Amy Foley

Creative Lead Live Tales
Becky Morris

Technical Production

Production Manager
Drummond Orr

Technician
Taylor Howie

Estates and Maintenance
Assistant
Ken Evans

Operations and Finance

Finance and Operations
Manager
Antony Robertson

Finance and Payroll Officer
Catherine Moody

Fundraising and Development
Manager
Alison Nicholson

Marketing and Communications

Marketing and Communications
Manager
Lisa Campbell

Marketing and Communications
Officer
Arthur Roberts

Marketing and Communications
Manager
Michele McCallion

Customer Services and Box Office

House and Estates Manager
Kirsten Dixon

Ruth Sheldon

Customer Service Assistants
Amy Becke

Deputy House and Estates
Managers
Michael Davies
Patrycja Nowacka

Hope Brown-King
Elisha Ewing
Elspeth Frith
Lukas Gabryseh

Duty Manager and Bar
Supervisors
Alicia Meehan
Sarah Matthews

Nathan Jones
Reece Lumsden
Bridget Marumo
Sidney Moshe Phoebus

Duty Manager and Bar
Supervisors
Jake Wilson Craw
Caitlin Fairlamb
Tyler Gatenby

Isabella Seale
Kathryn Watt

Box Office Assistants
Daniel Ball
Asa Beckett
Steven Blackshaw

Customer Services Assistants
and Bar Supervisors
Hannah Guthrie
Owen Saunders
Hendrika Seguro-Bigg

Joseph Duffy
Ruby Taylor
Jasper Wilding

Housekeeping

Housekeeping
Wendy Denny

Housekeeping
Angela Salem

Housekeeping
Lydia Igbinosa

Housekeeping
Camille Vitorino-Itoua

Champion

Scene One

The radio/cassette player is playing a Bollywood song: **Ham Kale Hey Toh Kya Huwa**.

Sheila   You know what he's saying here . . . he's saying . . . 'just because I'm black doesn't mean you can't love me'.

Azeem (15) *enters, he wears a shalwar kameez and a taqiyah, and he carries two pots, different sizes.*

Sheila (40s) *also wears a shalwar kameez. She watches him a moment with an amused smile. She has a mug, which she sips at throughout the scene.*

Sheila   He won't even care.

Azeem   I'm going to show him.

He indicates the pots, 'which one?'. **Sheila** *indicates one with a nod.* **Azeem** *leaves and a moment later returns with a chopping board and some onions. He sits and gingerly starts to peel the onions.*

Sheila   Do you want me to do it?

Azeem   No! I'm going to show him.

Sheila   Don't let him wind you up.

Azeem   You let him wind you up.

Sheila   That's different.

Azeem   How's it different?

Beat.

Sheila   Don't forget the garlic.

Azeem   I know! I know!

Sheila   There's no need to get mad at me . . . I've told you I'll do it for you.

Azeem   He'll know won't he?

Sheila   I'll make it a bit shit.

Azeem *stops what he is doing and looks at his mum 'not funny!'.*
Sheila *is amused. She comes over to him and puts her mug down.*
She tries to take over. **Azeem** *snatches his hand away.*

Azeem   I'll do it!

Sheila   Calm down . . . I'm trying to bloody help you.

Sheila *goes to find the garlic instead.*

Azeem   How many?

Sheila   Two should do you.

Azeem *grabs another onion and starts to peel it.*

Sheila   Here's the garlic . . . make sure you peel it.

Azeem   I'm not stupid!

Sheila *puts the garlic beside him.*

Sheila   You don't have to cut the onions so small.

Azeem *adjusts his chopping accordingly.*

Sheila   How was your day?

Azeem   Mr Burden said that if I finish before the rest, I
should pretend that I'm still working because it makes the
other boys feel stupid . . .

Sheila   They should feel stupid . . . you're ten times
cleverer than anyone at that school . . . including that bloody
Burden . . . did you speak to him about your A levels?

Azeem   I don't know, Mam.

Sheila   What do you mean 'you don't know'?

Azeem   It's only the posh kids that they encourage to go for
their A levels, and go to university.

Sheila   I don't bloody care who they encourage and what
they want . . . my boy is going to be a something and I'm not
going to let that bloody lot stop him!

Azeem *looks a bit sheepish.*

Azeem   I just thought that there may be something else.

Sheila   Something else? Are you going to be a chef? You'll end up like the rest of them . . . Back-breaking work for nothing . . . hired one day . . . sacked the next . . . because that's what it's going to be for you, you know.

Beat.

Sheila   I thought you said that one of them was really encouraging . . . who is that?

Azeem   Mr Clarke.

Sheila   Go and talk to him . . . tell him you want to do your A levels . . . that you want to go to medical school . . . he'll help you I'm sure.

Azeem   But there are load of lads that don't want to . . .

Sheila   Let those lads get their apprenticeships . . .

Azeem   Some of them can't even get that, Mam . . . you've got to know someone who'll get you one . . . like a dad or a brother who already works there.

Sheila   And who have you got that's going to get that for you . . . if you don't follow your dream . . . you'll end up with nothing . . . don't you want to follow your dream?

Azeem   I do, Mam . . . but it's not that simple is it?

Sheila   Go for what you want and don't let anything, or anyone stand in your way, like I did.

Azeem   What if they say no?

Sheila   I won't fucking let them!

Azeem *looks pointedly at the mug.*

Azeem   You might want to take it easy on that.

Sheila   It's nothing to do with this you little shit! You'll find out one day when you've got your own kids . . . how important they are to you . . . despite them being ungrateful sods.

Azeem   I should have a plan B.

Sheila   You can do it, Azeem . . . you've got more brains than any of them and you can graft harder than any of them . . . don't waste that opportunity son.

A reluctant **Azeem** *gives a nod of the head. He's chopped the onions, he looks at his mum, who nods towards the pot. He adds the onions and starts peeling the garlic. He struggles.*

Sheila   Why are you even doing this . . . he'll make it when he gets here.

Azeem   He does it deliberately . . . has us waiting around for him . . .

Sheila   You know he likes doing the cooking . . .

Azeem   He's always going on about his stupid curries . . .

Sheila   I don't see you complaining when you're eating them.

Azeem   He makes such a big deal about it . . . 'taste that' . . . 'the best curry you're ever going to eat' . . . that's all he goes on about . . . and then things like . . . 'stay out of the kitchen . . . I've got a system' a system . . . it's a kitchen . . . you're making curry . . . it's not rocket science.

Sheila   Well looking at a clip of you it might as well be.

Azeem   I can do this . . . and watch . . . he's going to be devastated.

Sheila   It's only curry.

Azeem   It's not 'only curry' Mam.

Sheila *watches him a beat.*

Sheila   What's brought all this on?

Azeem   Nowt.

Sheila   Come on Azeem, tell me . . . what's he done?

Azeem *hesitates.*

Azeem   He's just a dickhead Mam!

Sheila   Has he been picking on you again?

Azeem   He's always picking on me.

Sheila   What did he do?

Azeem *remains silent.*

Sheila   Tell me . . . what did he do?

Azeem   I was watching telly last night and he comes in and starts telling me to turn it over . . .

Sheila   Where was I?

Azeem   You were in the bath . . . and he's saying turn it over . . . but why should I . . . can't I watch what I want to watch?

Sheila   You watch some shit programmes though Azeem.

Azeem   Whose side are you on!

Sheila   I'm not on anyone's side.

Azeem   Doesn't sound like it.

Sheila   What were you watching?

Azeem   Doesn't matter what I was watching . . . that's not the point Mam . . . I should be able to watch what I want . . . I don't complain when you lot watch what you want to watch.

Sheila   Yes you bloody do!

Azeem   I hardly watch telly Mam . . . there's only a couple of things I like on there . . .

Sheila   You were watching *Mastermind* weren't you?

Azeem   So what! Better than *Match of the Day*! I like it . . . just because he can't answer any of the questions . . . it's not fair . . . me and . . . doesn't matter . . .

Azeem *is starting to well up, he turns his back on his mum so she can't see it.*

Sheila   Don't let him upset you.

Azeem *gathers himself, his indignation returning.*

Azeem   He is an idiot! He's denser than a black hole!

Like a good mother, **Sheila** *lets* **Azeem** *vent.*

Azeem   This onion's got more brains than him! At least an onion has layers . . . he's just thick all the way through!

Sheila   You're right son.

Azeem   I'm surprised he can tie his own laces!

Sheila   I know.

Azeem   When he bought those boots, he had to do a two-week induction course so he could lace them up.

Sheila *laughs.*

Sheila   That's funny.

Azeem *can't help but laugh, a bit calmer now.*

Sheila   So, what did he do?

Azeem *doesn't answer.*

Sheila   Please yourself . . . if you don't want to tell me, don't.

Azeem   He grabbed me, pulled me off the sofa . . . pinned me down and farted in my face Mam!

Sheila *bursts out laughing.*

Sheila   That's something our Mary would do . . . the dirty cow!

Azeem   Don't laugh!

Sheila   I'm sorry . . . that's disgusting . . . wait till he gets in . . . I'm going to tell him!

Azeem   No! I don't want you to say anything to him . . . he'll start calling me a grass and mammy's boy and all that . . . I can do it myself . . . I'm going to show him!

Azeem *has finished chopping the garlic – he adds it to the pot.*

Azeem   What do I do next?

Sheila   You want to add some salt . . . the salt will help the onions soften . . . about a spoonful.

Azeem *grabs a teaspoon.*

Sheila   Not that you silly sod . . . a tablespoon.

Azeem   Well I don't know do I!

Azeem *grabs the tablespoon, he heaps the spoon with salt.*

Sheila   Not that much! What are you trying to do . . . kill us!

Azeem   Well be precise then . . . what does 'about a spoonful' mean . . . you said spoonful . . . that's a spoonful.

Sheila   Less than that.

Azeem *lessens the salt on the spoon and shows his mum.*

Sheila   Remember, you can always add more, but if you put too much in you'll ruin it.

He shows her again. She nods. He adds it to the mix.

Sheila   Now put it on a low heat . . . and leave it.

Azeem *does as he is instructed.*

Sheila   Is your school doing anything for The Queen?

Azeem   I think the first and second years are making bunting and flags in art.

Sheila   Do you think we should do something?

Azeem   Invite her around for one of my curries.

Sheila   I'm being serious.

Azeem   What are *we* going to do, Mam?

Sheila   I don't know . . . there are street parties and all sorts going on . . . maybe we should organise something.

Azeem   You want to organise something . . . you?

Sheila   Why not me?

Azeem   You haven't been out of the house for a year.

Sheila   Yes I have!

Azeem   The off-licence doesn't count, Mam.

Beat.

Sheila   I was watching the Tyne Tees news and they were saying there are all sorts of things organised . . . they're arriving in her boat.

Azeem   It's a yacht.

Sheila   Boat, yacht, same thing, anyway, her and Prince Philip are arriving in their yacht and then they're going to make their way here . . . the streets are going to be lined with well-wishers they reckon . . . they said people shouldn't stand on the bridge when the boat comes in . . . good luck with that . . . and then she's going to have a walk around here in Shields . . . who'd have thunk it . . . The Queen in South Shields . . . walking around Gypsies Green.

Azeem   Where else is she going?

Sheila   Sunderland and Washington.

Azeem   All the highlights then.

Sheila   Well she has to doesn't she . . . wouldn't look good if she went to the Civic Centre and buggered off . . . I wonder why she's coming by boat?

Azeem   It's a floating palace . . . that's why Mam.

Beat.

Sheila   Can't be easy though.

Azeem   Being The Queen?

Sheila   Yeah . . . I'm sure she has her problems . . . like the rest of us.

Azeem   Yeah, like will someone nick my boat if I leave it here!

They both laugh.

Sheila   It's a yacht! I wonder if she's ever sad.

Azeem   What's she got to be sad about . . . she's The Queen.

Sheila   I know, but still.

Azeem   She's probably sad when she sees a clip of Charlie's ears.

Sheila   You know what I mean, Azeem.

They both fall silent a moment.

Azeem   I didn't think you'd be that bothered.

Sheila   I'm not.

Azeem   You want to organise a street party!

Sheila   Give the pot a stir . . . make sure the onions don't catch.

Azeem *stirs the pot.*

Sheila   I just think it's an occasion isn't it . . . The Queen . . . here . . . we won't see anything like that again will we?

Azeem   She might like it up here . . . come up every year
for Christmas to see Fenwick's window.

Sheila   They go to Balmoral at Christmas.

Azeem   You're full of Royal family knowledge aren't you.

Sheila   She's all over the telly this year isn't she . . . yeah, all
the kids are there . . . her mam . . . see that's nice . . . the way
she looks after her mam.

Azeem   I don't think she's the one who looks after her . . .
they'll have staff for that.

Sheila   It's not about the staff is it . . . it's about being a part
of the family . . . about her mam not feeling all alone . . . I
like that . . . she's done right by her.

Azeem   I don't think it works like that . . . she wasn't going
to stick her in her an old people's home, was she?

Sheila   God forbid! That would be awful . . . to be all alone
like that.

Sheila *goes to the pot and stirs it – lost in thought.*

Billy (18) *enters unnoticed. He wears jeans, Doc Martens and a
Crombie. He carries a sports holdall. He's annoyed that they're in
'his space'.*

Billy   What are you doing?

Sheila   Where have you been?

Billy   What are you doing in the kitchen?

Sheila   It's the kitchen . . . we're cooking.

Billy   I know it's the kitchen . . . I've told you I've got a
system . . . you better have not messed my system up.

Sheila   Azeem wanted to learn how to cook a curry.

Billy   Well I'm here now . . . I'll do it.

Sheila   Let Azeem do it.

Billy   He can't cook!

Sheila   He's learning!

Billy   He can learn somewhere else . . . I don't grab Dad's camera off him and say I want to be David fucking Bailey . . . this is my kitchen.

Sheila   Actually . . . you'll find it's my bloody kitchen and he has as much right to be in here as you.

Billy   He's going to mess everything up!

Sheila   I'll make sure he cleans up after he's finished.

Billy   I don't mean that! He'll be in here all the bloody time . . . you know what he's like . . . fucking *Mastermind*!

Sheila   And yeah you!

Azeem   Mam!

Sheila   Why did you fart in his face? That's disgusting!

Billy *laughs.*

Billy   It was an accident.

Azeem   No it bloody wasn't!

Billy   I'd had gobi allo . . . you know I get gassy when I've had cauliflower and potato.

Azeem   He's lying Mam!

Billy   Aw go running to mammy . . . you little grass . . . it was only a laugh.

Azeem   I thought you said it was an accident.

Beat.

Billy   It was an accident . . . that was funny.

Sheila   Bilal . . . don't ever do that again . . .

Billy   Alright I won't.

Sheila   Say sorry to your brother.

Billy   I'm not saying sorry to that little shit!

Sheila   Bilal! Say sorry! I mean it!

Beat.

Billy *goes to* **Azeem**, *he puts out his hand.*

Billy   Sorry . . . mates?

Azeem *refuses to shake hands.* **Billy** *looks at his mam, 'I'm trying'.*

Sheila   Shake his hand Azeem.

Azeem *reluctantly goes to shake* **Billy**'s *hand. But as he does,* **Billy** *pulls his hand away.*

Billy   Ahh dickhead!

Sheila   Bilal!

Billy   I'm only having a laugh with him . . . here, I got you something Mam.

He goes into his pocket and pulls out a beautiful small antique hand bell. He tinkles it. He hands it to his mum, with a peck on the cheek. **Sheila** *looks at it, a little perplexed.*

Sheila   What is it?

Billy   It's a prezzie.

Sheila   I know that . . . but what am I going to do with it?

Billy   'Aww thank you Bilal . . . that's lovely . . . very thoughtful of you.'

Sheila   Sorry . . . thank you . . . I just don't know what I'm supposed to do with it.

Billy   Don't do anything with it . . . it's just something that I thought was beautiful and I thought of you . . . so I got it for you.

Azeem   Creep.

Sheila   That's very kind . . . where did you get it?

Billy   An antique shop.

Azeem   What are you doing in antique shops?

Billy   I was walking past, and I seen it in the window.

Sheila   How much was it?

Billy   Doesn't matter how much it was . . . I got it for you.

Sheila   Where did you get the money to buy an antique?

Billy   Can't you just say thank you?

Azeem   It must have been expensive, it's an antique.

Billy   Just because it's in an antique shop doesn't mean it was expensive.

Azeem   So it was a second-hand shop.

Billy   No! It was an antique shop!

Azeem   Technically, an antique shop is a second-hand shop.

Billy   Technically . . . you're a dickhead who's about to get laid out!

Sheila   Stop it, the pair of you!

Billy   Well tell your little angel then!

Sheila   Enough!

Billy *looks at the pot and then at* **Sheila***.*

Billy   Shall I take over . . . that coriander I planted is ready to use . . . I'll whack some in . . . it'll be gorgeous.

Sheila *nods.*

Azeem   Mam!

Sheila   I'm starving Azeem . . . and your brother does a lovely chicken curry . . .

Billy   I'll bang some peas in as well Mam, you love a choosa mhatter.

Azeem   I was supposed to be doing that!

Sheila   We'll get you started on some dal . . . dal will be an easy one for you to learn . . . and if you mess it up we won't have to bin a full chicken.

Billy *takes off his coat. He is now in his element. He first looks in the pot, has a sniff and a stir. He looks at the flame and adjusts it slightly, probably just for effect.*

Billy   Wait 'till I tell you this news . . .

Sheila   About The Queen?

Billy   That's not news . . . that's fish and chip wrapping . . . and anyway who cares about The Queen?

Azeem   Mam wants to organise a street party.

Billy   Throw a street party for her? Why? Just some toff making sure the peasants don't get out of hand.

Sheila   She's not a toff . . . she's The Queen!

Billy   She's the head of the toffs . . . what's she ever done for us . . . she lives in a palace . . . doesn't have a care in the world . . .

Sheila   Of course she does . . . everyone has worries . . . she's no different.

Billy   I've seen how these people live . . .

Azeem   How do you know how these people live?

Billy   Those big stately houses . . . full of expensive stuff . . . paintings worth thousands . . . chairs . . . I kid you not . . . chairs that cost thousands of pounds . . . what have they got to worry about?

Sheila   She's coming here to Shields . . . that's something.

Billy   She's going everywhere . . . someone has chosen where she goes . . . given her a list . . . 'It's the North-East today ma'am', 'oh really . . . is that where those creatures spend their time underground digging for coal?', 'yes ma'am . . . apparently they make ships as well ma'am'. What a load of bollocks! And those saps . . . stood on the streets . . . waving their little flags . . . for what? For her? I don't fucking think so.

Sheila   What's got into you?

Billy   I'm sick of the sight of it Mam, everywhere you go . . . The Queen this . . . The Queen that . . . nah . . . I've got some proper news . . . listen to this . . . listen to this . . . so I'm in the gym, on the pads . . . and Mickey's taking the sessions . . . which is unusual . . . then Johnny . . .

Sheila   You're just hitting me with names . . . who's Mickey?

Billy   Mickey is Johnny's assistant.

Sheila   And who's Johnny?

Billy   Johnny Walker, he runs the club . . . he comes out carrying a suitcase, all dolled up . . . and he calls all the lads together for a photograph . . . so we're all in this photo, you know, stood around the ring and that . . . then he says he's going to show Muhammad Ali the picture he just took . . .. and then he says . . . he's going to America to get Muhammad Ali . . .

Azeem   Get him for what?

Billy   Get him to come here . . . to come to South Shields . . . to help raise money for the boys' club . . . not just ours . . . others as well.

Sheila   Muhammad Ali isn't going to come to South Shields.

Billy   Why not?

Sheila   Why would he want to come here?

Billy   To help people . . . not like The Queen . . . he's the people's champion . . . Johnny's gone over there to tell him that they need funds for the boys' clubs . . . he's going to do something for the people . . . he's like that.

Sheila   You don't know what he's like.

Billy   You don't know what The Queen is like but you want to throw her a party . . . for what . . . because she was born into the right family . . . Muhammad Ali stands for something . . . he's done something . . . off his own back . . . rags to riches.

Sheila   I hated those bloody fights . . . He's just a massive attention seeker . . . isn't he Azeem?

Azeem   I couldn't care less . . . any fool can punch someone in the head.

Billy   Well why don't you go and try it . . . see where it gets you . . . everyone loves Muhammad Ali.

Sheila   Not everyone . . .

Billy   You watch . . . if he comes here . . . the streets will be packed . . . they're already talking about exhibition fights . . . a walk about . . . meeting with the people . . . it's going to be class.

Sheila   If . . . if he comes . . . but I'll tell you now . . . he won't be coming here . . . I hope he doesn't . . .

Billy   Why do you have to be such a downer?

Sheila   I'm not . . . I'm just saying I can't see him coming here.

Billy   You're always like that.

Sheila   Like what?

Billy   Miserable.

Azeem   No she's not.

Billy   Must be me then . . . coz she's miserable every time I'm around.

Sheila   No I'm not! I'm trying my hardest . . . and you don't care.

Billy   You need to get a grip of yourself.

Sheila   What do you mean 'get a grip of myself'?!

Azeem   Mam . . . it's alright . . .

Billy   We do . . . all of us.

Azeem   Will you shut up!

Billy   I'm just saying it how it is . . . Ali coming here is a good thing.

Sheila   I hate Muhammad Ali! . . . I hope he gets battered!

Sheila *aggressively drains her mug.*

Lights fade.

Scene Two

Billy *stands alone in the centre of the stage, a mic descends, he takes it like he's a ring announcer.*

Billy   Ladies and gentlemen, welcome to the MAIN EVENT of the night!

Innnn the blue corner . . . fighting out of South Shields, England! With an unbeaten record in snide comments and just two big losses in life – everything she's said and everything she's done – it's *Shhhheeeilaaaa!* She can bring the mood down faster that you can say 'anti-depressant'.

Pissed and pissed off . . . Sheila steps into the ring tonight as the reigning champion of holding a grudge. Her best move? *Dredging things up that happened years ago!*

And watch out – if Sheila lands her guilt-trip punch, you'll see more canvas than Van Gogh.

But don't be fooled, folks. Sheila's strength isn't just in the punches – she knows how to keep going, hitting the same nerve again and again. The big question is, will she stay on top forever? Or will she finally face her toughest opponent yet . . . her own happiness?

And now . . . *drumroll, please! Innnnn* the red corner . . . weighing slightly less than all the pressure Mam's put on him, and fighting out of Cloud Cuckoo Land, with a record of disappointing no one but himself . . . It's *Azeeeeeem, 'The Thinking Man!'. Zero friends, zero craic and zero personality.*

This lad's got potential, folks. He can think his way out of any fight – and straight into a corner! His best move? *The Sorry Shuffle!* And when it comes to running away from confrontation, no one's quicker on their feet. Azeem's spent his career dodging punches – from life, from Mam, and even from himself. However, in the safety of his own home he's unstoppable!

But don't write him off just yet. His secret weapon? Brain Power! Azeem's got a sharp mind that could do wonders – if only he'd stop second-guessing himself long enough to use it. Will this be the moment Azeem finally proves he's more than just a waste of space? Or will he fall apart like a wet paper bag?

IIIT'S TIME TOOOO FIIIIIGHTTTTT!

Scene Three

In the living room **Sheila** *is sat in front of the TV attaching bunting onto a piece of string. She wears a shalwar kameez. She sips from her mug.*

The news is on.

Newscaster   *Her Majesty The Queen's Jubilee tour continues unabated, The Queen and Prince Philip today witnessed a parade in their honour. It included a flyover by the Air Force with both fixed wing and propeller aircraft . . .*

She pricks her finger with the needle.

Sheila   Ahhh! Ya bastard!

Azeem *enters in salwar kameez and a taqiyah. He goes and picks up a camera. He fiddles with it throughout the scene.*

Azeem   How many Hail Marys is that?

Sheila   Not as many Allah Wakbars ya little shit . . .

Billy   Where is she?

Sheila   God knows . . . how was Mosque?

Azeem   Everyone was talking about this Ali thing.

Sheila   I bet they're loving it down there . . . and St Hilda's has got The Queen coming . . . all we need now is for the Pope to turn up and say Mass at St Bede's and we'll have a full set.

Azeem   Half of them think he's not going to come . . .

Sheila   Who . . . the Pope?

Azeem   Very funny, Mam . . . the other half want to give the Mosque a new coat of paint . . . meanwhile no one knows if this Johnny Walker's even met with Ali yet.

Sheila   He's not coming . . . and daft arse is going to be as sick as a parrot . . . serves him right.

Azeem   That's a bit harsh.

Sheila   Are you two pals now?

Azeem   No I'm just saying . . . he'd love it.

Sheila   I'd love a win on the Pools . . . not going to happen though.

Azeem   You don't play the Pools.

She takes a sip from her mug.

Azeem   On it again?

Sheila   Just a cheeky one.

Azeem   Is it alright if I have a bit?

Sheila   Don't you dare!

Beat.

Sheila   Anyway, it won't be good if you go to the Mosque smelling like you've just fallen out of The Mechanics Arms . . . I get bored sat in here all day on my own.

Azeem   Get yourself out . . . Mrs Al-Kamadi was asking after you the other day.

Sheila   What was she saying?

Azeem   She was just saying that she hadn't seen you for ages . . . that you should call around sometime . . . she said she'd called around here a couple of times but no one answered the door.

Sheila   I must have been cleaning or something.

Azeem   I told her you hardly go anywhere . . . that she'll catch you sooner or later.

Sheila   What did you tell her that for? I don't want her coming around here.

Azeem   I thought you two were friends.

Sheila   She'll be around all the bloody time . . . dragging me to the Mosque . . .

Azeem   What's wrong with that? You've stopped praying as well.

Sheila   I say Hail Marys instead.

She laughs.

Azeem   Mam!

Sheila   I'll get back to it.

Azeem   When? It might help.

Sheila   God doesn't help . . . God just makes your life miserable.

Azeem   The imam was saying that God will never give you a test that you can't overcome . . . it is the choices you make in overcoming that test that are being observed.

Sheila   Well here's a choice . . . I'm not getting dragged to that bloody women's group by her.

Azeem   Why not?

Sheila   Because she's a nosy cow! That's why!

Azeem   All she did was ask how you were.

Sheila   You don't know what people are like . . . you're only a kid . . . they're horrible . . . the lot of them . . . you shouldn't tell people stuff about me.

Azeem   You should get out of the house.

Sheila   Are you telling me what to do now?

Azeem   It was a suggestion.

Sheila   Here's a suggestion . . . mind your own bloody business.

Sheila *immediately regrets saying this*.

Sorry . . . I didn't mean that . . . I'm sorry.

Azeem   It's alright Mam . . . don't worry about it.

Sheila   You're a good son Azeem . . . here, do you want have a go at cooking some dal . . . I'll give you a hand . . . I've made the tea . . . but we can have a bash at some dal if you like.

Azeem   I'm alright . . . another time . . . I think I'll go up to my room.

Sheila   Don't go . . . stay . . . sit and talk to me . . . come on, sit down.

Azeem   Mam . . .

Sheila   Come on Azeem . . . we hardly talk anymore.

Azeem   We talk all the time.

Sheila   Come on, sit down . . . tell me about your day.

Azeem   I'll sit if you tell me about your day.

Sheila   Okay.

Azeem *sits.*

Sheila   I got up . . . I went and did my cleaning round . . . came in and sorted the house . . . I've put your undies and your socks on your bed . . . you got your photographs developed . . . they're brilliant, them . . . how come you didn't show me?

Azeem   I was going to.

Sheila   You kept that quiet . . . anyway . . . I made something for tea . . . then I watched a bit of telly . . . *Pebble Mill* . . . they did this thing on how to make bunting . . . so I've been doing that all afternoon . . . I've had more pricks than . . . doesn't matter . . . really it was like every other day . . . a bit shit.

Azeem   That's what I mean . . . get out of the house . . . go somewhere . . . do something.

Sheila   I will . . . when I'm ready.

Azeem   It's been a year.

Beat.

Sheila   Is that what your brother told you to say?

Azeem   He didn't tell me to say anything . . . I wouldn't listen to him anyway.

Sheila   That's what he wants . . . for us all to move on . . . always going on about it . . . he's always had a bloody mouth on him . . . no consideration for other people . . . just says anything that comes into his head . . . to hell with the consequences.

Azeem   I wish I was like that sometimes.

Sheila   That's all I bloody need!

Azeem   I just wish I'd . . . you know . . .

Sheila   No . . . I don't bloody know . . .

Azeem   You're not listening to what I'm saying Mam . . . you never do.

Sheila   I'm always listening to what you say . . . I do whatever you want . . . your brother thinks I do nothing else.

Azeem   You know what . . . it doesn't matter . . .

Sheila   Explain . . . what do you mean?

Azeem   He can't help himself . . . I . . .

Sheila   Well he should bloody well learn . . . there's a lot of things I could say to him . . . some home truths . . . I hold my tongue . . . but one of these days . . . he's going to get as good as he gives and he's not going to like it.

Azeem   Just leave it Mam.

Sheila   Why should I?

Azeem   Coz' you're Mam . . . and that's what mams do.

Sheila   And the bloody rest and what thanks do we get for it.

Azeem   It's going to be alright . . .

Sheila   Is it though, Azeem . . . you say that but you don't know what it's like.

Azeem   It's the same for all of us.

Sheila   Doesn't feel like that . . . It feels like everyone else is alright and I'm fucked.

Azeem   Mam.

Sheila   What?

Azeem   When you're on that stuff . . . you swear like anything.

Sheila   You must be the only teenager in the world that doesn't swear.

Azeem   I swear . . . when it's appropriate to swear.

Sheila   You'd have been having kittens if you grew up in our house.

Azeem   I didn't grow up in a house like that though.

Sheila   Just as well . . . if you think this is bad . . . you should have heard our Mary.

Azeem   I can only imagine.

Beat.

Sheila   Don't be like that.

Azeem   Like what?

Sheila   Like you're the clever one and we're all stupid.

Azeem   I think the word you're looking for is condescending.

Sheila   You know what . . .

Azeem   What? . . . I was only telling you what the word was.

Sheila *leaves.*

Billy *enters his house with the painting under his arm.*

Azeem   What's that?

Billy   A thing of beauty . . . where's Mam?

Azeem   She's putting the tea on . . . what have you got?

Billy *puts the painting down and unwraps it.*

Azeem   That *is* beautiful . . . where did you get it?

Billy   I thought you'd like it.

Azeem   Is it for me?

Billy   Don't be daft!

Azeem   Where did you get it?

Billy   I seen it in a second-hand shop . . . thought that's worth something that . . . so I took a little punt.

Azeem   Is that what you do?

Billy   Something like that.

Azeem   How?

Billy   What do you mean how?

Azeem   Like, how?

Billy *looks* **Azeem** *up and down.*

Billy   For a start I don't dress like Ali fucking Baba!

He starts to wrap the picture back up.

Azeem   That's preposterous . . .

Billy *bursts out laughing.*

Billy   Fucking preposterous!

He is still laughing when **Sheila** *enters.*

Billy   Have you heard what he's just said Mam . . . he said I was preposterous.

Sheila   He's been condescending since he got in.

Sheila   Where have you been?

Billy   Out.

Sheila   Out where?

Billy   Out with my mates.

Sheila   Which mates?

Billy   You don't know them.

Sheila   That's because you never bring them around here
. . . never have.

Azeem   His mates are those lads that hang around on
Frederick Street . . . I've seen him.

Sheila   Fredrick Street?

Billy   They're good lads.

Sheila   They're a bunch of thugs . . . there's a swatstika
painted on the walls and all sorts down there . . .

Billy   What are you going down there for . . .

Sheila   Yeah, why are you going down there for?

Billy   Did you go dressed like that?

Azeem   No.

Billy   Don't leave the house looking like that, it's
embarrassing.

Sheila   He can leave the house however he wants.

Billy   He's got a target on his back.

Sheila   Why are either of you going down there for?

Billy   It's bad enough as it is and then you've got him
dressed like that . . . and you . . . why do you still wear that
clobber?

Azeem   She doesn't make me dress like this . . . I was at
Mosque.

Billy   What are you sending him there for?

Sheila   You used to go.

Billy   Waste of time.

Azeem   She's not sending me, I go because I want to.

Billy   What a waste of time . . . get yourself out . . . get a girlfriend . . . listen to music . . . be fucking normal.

Sheila   Normal . . . like you? Out all hours of the day . . . God knows what you're getting up to . . . you can't even find yourself a job.

Azeem   But he's always got new clothes on Mam.

Sheila   Where are you getting the money for those new clothes?

Billy   Don't worry about me . . . I'm going to be alright . . .

Sheila   How? How are you going to be alright . . . you should be out there looking for a job.

Billy   That ship has sailed hasn't it?

Sheila   And whose fault is that?

Azeem   Why can't you get a job?

Billy   None of your business!

Sheila   You can still try . . . there'll be something.

Billy   I aren't going to be stuck doing someone else's bidding . . . that's for chumps . . . I'll find something that suits me.

Sheila   And what's that going to be? Do you think likes of us get jobs that suit us? You have to go out there and graft . . . put the hours in . . . like your dad did . . . how are you going to lead a respectable life if you haven't got a job?

Billy   Maybe I don't want to live a respectable life . . .
maybe I want to do what I want to do . . . and not give a fuck
what people think.

Sheila   What would your dad think . . .?

Billy   Doesn't matter what he would think . . . he's not here
is he . . . it's up to us to make a life without him now.

Sheila   He wanted you both to achieve something in life.

Billy   I am going to achieve something in life. Anyway,
doesn't matter though does it . . . he's left us.

Sheila   He didn't leave us!

Scene Four

The family are sat watching the telly. **Sheila** *is resentful as she sips
at her mug,* **Billy** *sits in anticipation,* **Azeem** *fiddles with a camera.*

Interviewer   Time Magazine *once wrote of our guest tonight,
'He is Hercules struggling through the twelve labours. He is Jason
chasing the Golden Fleece. He is Galahad, Serrano, D'Artagnan.
When he scowls, strong men shudder, and when he smiles, women
swoon. He is without doubt the most beautiful and complete athlete
I've ever seen, to others he is a political leader, yet to more people
who care very little about sport and even less about politics he's one
of the world's great entertainers. A character, a comedian and a
sometime poet.' Here he is in all his splendour. Ladies and gentlemen
. . . Muhammad Ali!*

Sheila   Do we have to watch this rubbish again?

Billy   You love a chat show.

Sheila   I like chat shows, it's him I can't stand.

Billy   You don't have to hang around . . . you can go you
know.

Sheila   Go where?

Billy   To bed.

Sheila   I'm not going to bed at this time!

Billy   Suit yourself . . . 'Ere dickhead, put that down and watch this, you might learn something.

Azeem   You're alright.

Billy   You won't get any of this in your poncey grammar school.

Sheila   He gets a proper education in that place, not like this rubbish he's spouting.

Billy   It's the truth.

Sheila   How would you know what the truth is . . .?

Billy   I know Mam . . . you know . . . you've lived it.

Sheila   *Silence*.

Billy   Listen to him . . . get some inspiration.

Sheila   I'd rather set my hair on fire.

Billy   Might be an improvement.

Sheila   What's wrong with my hair like!

Azeem   There's nothing wrong with your hair Mam.

Sheila *finds a compact and inspects her hair.* **Billy** *has a smile on his face.*

Billy   See the thing about Ali people don't understand is, he's a man of peace.

Sheila   That's what your dad used to say . . . I'd say if he was for peace he wouldn't be saying the stuff he says . . .

Billy   Can't make an omelette without breaking a few eggs Mam.

Sheila   He knows . . . he knows if he spouts that rubbish he'll get more people to follow him . . .

Billy   That's not true . . . he doesn't say things so that people will follow him . . . people follow him because of the things he says . . .

Azeem   Wow . . . profound.

Sheila   You can't do that . . . set one lot of people off against another . . . it just makes it worse.

Billy   So you're saying that everything is hunky dory.

Sheila   Of course it's not . . . but if you really want peace . . . you'd be like that other fella . . . what's his name . . . the one they shot . . .

Azeem   Gandhi?

Sheila   No, the other one.

Billy   Malcolm X?

Sheila   No . . . the other one, you know, the other one who they shot.

Azeem   Martin Luther King.

Sheila   Yeah, him.

Billy   He was a fool . . . he was like let them keep slapping you and sooner or later they'll get tired and stop . . . yeah right!

Sheila   What would you do clever arse?

Billy *impersonates Ali.*

Billy/Ali   *If the fool talk jive he's gonna fall in five.*

Azeem *laughs,* **Sheila** *gives an amused shake of the head.* **Billy** *warms to their reaction.*

Billy   I'm telling you . . . he's *the greatest of all time . . . the prettiest . . . he's so mean he makes medicine sick . . .*

Sheila   There are loads of interviews that are better than this.

Billy   That's because they're all . . . 'Then there was the time me and darling Cecil were sailing in the Med'.

Sheila   But that's what you want . . . a glimpse at a better life . . . whereas this . . . this is just him having a whinge . . . well we've all been through stuff . . . but some of us have just got on with it . . . we don't go spouting off all the time.

Billy   That's because nobody cares what you think.

Sheila   That sounds about right . . . they should ask him . . .

Sheila *impersonates the interviewer.*

Sheila/Interviewer   *Can I put this to you Muhammad . . . why have you had countless affairs and divorced a number of women?*

Azeem *starts laughing.*

Azeem   It's good that, Mam.

Billy *is not as amused.*

Sheila   I'm a woman of many talents, son . . .

Billy   Can we shush please . . .

Sheila *and* **Azeem** *share an amused look.*

Billy *is glued to the show.*

We go into a pastiche of Muhammad Ali interviews.

Ali is funny, provocative, poetic and challenging. He speaks about boxing, race, religion and politics. He is in turn charming, angry, reflective and insightful.

We end the sequence with Ali calling the white American man the devil.

Sheila   This is what I mean . . . look at him . . . sat on there . . . without a care in the world saying stuff like that . . . calling people devils . . . what does he know?

Azeem   He said it all there like.

Billy *reverts back to himself.*

Billy   He's brilliant isn't he . . . I told ya!

Sheila   Rubbish.

Beat.

Billy   Are your family devils, Mam?

Sheila   What type of question is that?

Azeem   You're a dickhead you!

Billy   What?

Billy   But we've never met them so we wouldn't know.

Sheila   Why do you do it Bilal?

Billy   Do what? And it's Billy.

Sheila   You know exactly what I mean . . . you're always pushing, pushing, pushing aren't you?

Billy   It was just a question.

Sheila   You're the devil . . . I know that.

Azeem   He's not talking about individuals . . . he's talking about societies.

Beat.

Sheila   They're all after power . . . anyone who gets a sniff of it gets obsessed with it . . . and they use the telly and the papers and the radio to play on people's fears . . . then say if we do it like the way I'm saying everything is going to be alright . . . is it hell!

Billy   People only respect brawn or money . . . if you can batter someone or have enough money to pay someone to batter them, people will respect you.

Sheila   What a load of rubbish . . . you earn respect . . . by your actions . . . your character.

Billy   Nobody cares about character, Mam . . . they're interested in what's in your pocket . . . whether you scare them.

Sheila   That's fear . . . people don't respect fear.

Billy   Maybe not . . . but they're too scared to say owt to you!

Beat.

Azeem   He made some good points there though . . . like, how can Jesus be white if he was born in Bethlehem . . . I'm going to ask Mr Gibbon in RE.

Sheila   Don't you dare!

Billy   Yeah don't say a word . . . you don't want to be upsetting those that will decide what your future's going to be . . . told you . . . listen to what he has to say . . . he'll change how you see the world . . . especially you.

Sheila   Why especially him?

Billy   Because Berty Big Brains is going stand out amongst those posh white folks and he needs to understand what's waiting for him.

Sheila   He's going to be a doctor . . . he's the one that's going to be telling other people what to do.

Billy   But there'll always be someone above him, won't there? . . . his boss.

Beat.

Azeem   Have you heard anything about whether he's coming or not?

Billy   They're still in negotiations.

Sheila *lets out a laugh.*

Sheila   Ha! A painter and decorator from Shields negotiating with Muhammad Ali . . . what a load of cobblers!

Billy   What would you know . . . you're off an estate.

Sheila   Shall I tell you what growing up on an estate does teach you . . . it teaches you to spot when someone's talking complete and utter shite!

Sheila *and* **Azeem** *laugh,* **Billy** *is not amused.*

Azeem   So what is the going price for getting the world heavyweight champion to come to South Shields?

Sheila *and* **Azeem** *keep on laughing at him. We can see* **Billy** *is seething now.*

Billy   Whatever the price, we need to have him here

Ali is asked about his fight for racial equality in America – Ali proclaims some stringent views around mixed marriages – which prompts **Sheila** *to get up and turn the TV off.*

Billy   What are you doing, I was watching that!

Sheila   I'm not having that in my house!

Billy   It's Muhammad Ali!

Sheila   He's talking about you! About us!

Billy   Just let me watch the telly . . .

Billy *makes a move to put the TV back on.* **Sheila** *stands in his way, defiant.*

Sheila   Don't you dare put that television on!

Azeem   That bit will be over now Mam.

Sheila   Shut up Azeem!

There's a stand off.

Billy   You don't like the truth do you?

Sheila   What do you mean by that?

Billy   Muhammad Ali talks some sense and you don't want to hear it.

Sheila   He's just said the white man is the devil . . . that bit's true.

Billy   I'm not going on about that.

Sheila   That's the only bit that matters to me.

Billy   Half-brown kinky haired, that's the bit that matters to me.

Sheila   I know that, I've known that since you were a kid . . . you've got the devil in you . . . like your grandparents and your aunties . . .

Billy   They're your mam and dad, they're your sisters.

Sheila   They're dead to me . . . good riddance to them.

Billy   Dead, like me dad.

Sheila   He was more of a human being than they could ever have been.

Billy   You married him just to piss them off.

Sheila   I loved him!

Billy   And they called you a Paki lover, is that it?

Sheila *punches* **Billy**.

Azeem   Mam!

Beat.

Billy *laughs a hollow laugh, goes and retrieves the painting and leaves.*

Scene Five

Azeem *stands in the middle of the stage – he looks a bit shell-shocked. The mic descends, he tentatively takes it.*

Azeem   Ladies and gentlemen . . . err, for tonight's . . . I mean . . . over there . . . in the red corner . . . I mean the blue corner . . .

He is lost for words.

Azeem   Sorry . . . can you give me a second . . .

There is a beat as **Azeem** *gathers himself.*

Azeem   Ladies and gentlemen . . . for tonight's main fight . . . sorry, sorry, sorry . . .

Sheila *enters the space.*

Sheila   Oh for God's sake Azeem, give it here . . .

She takes the mic and shoos **Azeem** *away.* **Azeem** *makes his exit in a downtrodden fashion.* **Sheila** *is now the ring announcer. She is melancholy in tone. A deep sadness imbues her words.*

Sheila   Ladies and gentlemen . . . welcome to tonight's bout . . . in the red corner we have my husband Sadiq . . . from Jhelum in Pakistan . . . he fought out of South Shields, in the North East of England.

He spent his career chainsmoking, working and keeping his head down. His favourite move was 'turn the other cheek'.

His training regime was dedication, hope and a burning desire for a better life for himself and his family.

Don't get me wrong, ladies and gentlemen – he wasn't perfect; stubborn as a mule, moody, he could be a right twat . . . but he was ours with every inch of his being.

In the blue corner . . . my family . . . from Galway in Ireland as they keep banging on about . . . and also fighting out of South Shields . . . God-fearing people as long as God is white and a Catholic.

Their favourite moves – bigotry and hypocrisy and endless gossip.

Their training regime – getting pissed, singing folk songs about the land they'd left behind and telling each other about the prejudices they faced and the oppression of their people.

Height, reach, weight almost identical, the difference in class . . . unmatchable.

And who in this world do you think won that fight?

Scene Six

Sheila *sews a Union Jack flag using material she has found around the house. It's a valiant effort, but not quite there.* **Sheila** *knows this.*

She looks at her watch, then towards the door. She goes back to assessing her sewing efforts.

After a moment **Azeem** *enters. He has his school pants and shirt on. He takes his camera from the bag.*

Sheila   Where have you been?

Azeem   How's the flag coming on?

Sheila   I don't think I have it right . . . where's your blazer and tie?

Azeem   In here. (*He indicates his bag.*)

Sheila   What have you got them in there for, you're going to crease them.

Sheila *takes his bag and pulls out the blazer and tie, as she does so, a magazine and some pamphlets also fall out.* **Azeem** *tries to get to them, but* **Sheila** *picks them up before he can. She shakes out the blazer and drapes it over the back of a chair, then looks at the literature.*

Sheila   What's all this?

Azeem   There was an open day at the art college . . . I went along.

Sheila   What are you going there for . . .?

Azeem   Just to see what it was like.

Sheila   Why?

Azeem   It's just art college.

Sheila   Don't give up on your dream, Azeem . . . you can't give in.

She notices something on one of the pamphlets.

Sheila   Sunderland! You went to Sunderland?

Azeem   It was only a bus ride away Mam.

Sheila   It's a different town! What are you doing going to a different town?

Azeem   It's only Sunderland, Mam, I'm not a kid anymore . . . I can go to Sunderland on my own.

Sheila *is taken aback by* **Azeem**'s *pushback.*

Sheila   I was just saying . . . it's a way away.

Azeem   It's not that far.

Sheila   But still . . . why would you want to go and see what art college was like? You're better than art college.

Beat.

Sheila   Why didn't you tell me you were going?

Azeem   You would have worried.

Sheila   But you should still tell me when you're doing things like this.

Azeem   I will next time.

Sheila   There's going to be a next time?

Azeem   I just went to see what it was like.

Sheila   And?

Azeem   And what?

Sheila   And what was it like?

Azeem   It was cool.

Sheila   Cool? What does that mean?

Azeem   It was good . . . there were loads of students there from all over . . . all sorts of people.

Sheila   Any that looked like you?

Beat.

Azeem   There's no one at my school that looks like me . . . anyway, no one seemed to care what I looked like.

Sheila   At medical college there'll be loads of people that look like you.

Azeem   But medical college, Mam.

Sheila   Well don't be a doctor, be an engineer, an accountant, a lawyer . . .

Billy   They were different, Mam.

Sheila   Different how?

Azeem   From all over, nobody from my school . . . but there was some there from Cleadon.

Sheila   Park?

Azeem   Cleadon Village.

Sheila   How do you know they were from Cleadon Village?

Azeem   I talked to them.

Sheila   What were they like?

Azeem   They were nice . . . there was three of them . . . a brother and sister, they're twins and their friend . . . they have a band.

Sheila   A band?

Azeem   Yeah, a music band . . . a punk band . . . here look . . . they're in that magazine.

He takes the magazine and shows her a picture.

Azeem   That's them . . . that's Gary . . . and that's Joanne, Jo, they're the twins . . .

Sheila   Not identical then.

Azeem   They're a boy and a girl Mam . . . and that's Derek . . . he plays drums . . . Gary plays guitar and Jo plays the bass.

Sheila   Does she now.

Azeem   There's no need to be sarky.

Sheila   I wasn't being sarky.

Azeem   Yes you were, they were nice.

Sheila   Those posh kids are taught how to be nice to people, even if they don't like them . . . and what have they got on . . . I wouldn't want to be seen dressed like that.

Azeem   It's a band, Mam, they supposed to wear fashionable clothes.

Sheila   Fashionable? They look like they've been dragged through a hedge.

Azeem   They've got a gig in a few weeks . . . at their village hall . . . said I should come along.

Sheila   Yeah, but you're not going to go are you . . . you'll have to take two buses . . . and you don't even like that type of music . . . you're not going to go, are you?

Beat.

Azeem   No . . . I don't think I will.

Sheila   Good boy . . . you wouldn't like it . . .

Azeem *is disappointed.*

Sheila   What do you want for your tea? I've ironed your shalwar kameez for you for Mosque.

Azeem   I'm not going.

Sheila   How come?

Azeem   I don't fancy it . . .

Beat.

Azeem   Why can't our kid get a job?

Sheila   He could if he tried . . . your dad managed . . .

Azeem   It doesn't sound like it . . . he always says . . . that you know why he can't get a job, why's that?

Beat.

Sheila   It's because he's got a criminal record.

Azeem   Our kid has, what for?

Sheila   Criminal damage.

Azeem   Really, what did he do?

Sheila   He threw bleach over some fella's garden . . . I can never understand why he did it . . . it doesn't make sense . . . . . . killed all his prize begonias . . . senseless . . . and he hasn't said until this day why. I can never understand him . . . why he would do something like that.

Azeem   Have you asked?

Sheila   Of, course, we both did . . . he just kept saying he just did it . . . didn't know why . . . he just did it . . . I don't understand you boys sometimes.

Azeem   Have you spoke to him . . . since . . .

Sheila   About the begonias?

Azeem   No, the argument . . .

Sheila   I haven't seen him . . . he comes in when we're asleep . . . And he leaves as soon as he wakes up . . . doesn't even come in here.

Azeem   Have you tried going to his room, you know when he's in there?

Beat.

Sheila   I haven't.

Azeem   But you're his mam.

Sheila   He's not a kid anymore . . .

Azeem   But . . .

Sheila   He said that word . . . how could he say that . . . him of all people.

Azeem   It doesn't matter what he said, Mam . . . he's my brother isn't he . . . I don't like it when it's like this.

Beat.

Sheila   Alright Azeem . . . alright . . . but I want you to do something for me . . . I want you to get this art college nonsense out of your head . . . I want you to follow your dream.

Beat.

Azeem   Alright Mam.

Sheila   Say kasme.

Azeem   Kasme koran knee.

Sheila *is pleased.*

Offstage we hear **Billy** . . . ***Ali Bumaye! Ali Bumaye! Ali Bumaye!**

Billy   Have you heard, kid? . . . Muhammad Ali is coming!

Billy *enters. He's a skinhead.*

Billy *has all the gear on . . . the 18-eye Doc Martens, the short jeans, the Fred Perry T-shirt, the braces.*

He carries some fish and chips wrapped in newspaper and an actual newspaper.

Azeem *is stopped in his tracks, lost for words.* **Billy** *is amused by the shock he's causing.*

Azeem *doesn't say anything.*

It's in the paper . . . I know . . . I told you he was coming . . . and what about this . . . he's coming the day after The Queen . . . staying for four days . . . they're still working out the finer details . . . but four days . . . it's going to be brilliant.

Sheila *enters, she is also stunned by* **Billy**'*s appearance.*

Sheila   What have you done?

Billy   I got some fish and chips . . . didn't fancy curry . . . anyone want some?

Sheila   No! We don't want your stupid fish and chips! What the hell do you think you're doing dressing like that?

Billy   Lots of lads dress like this.

Azeem   But . . .

Billy   Stop having kittens, they're only clothes.

Sheila   You're doing this to torment me aren't you!

Billy   I've got better things to do than to torment you.

Beat.

Billy   Will everyone calm down? . . . They're just clothes . . . it's just a haircut . . . Are you sure you don't fancy some?

Billy *sits down and starts to unwrap his food.*

Azeem   Why are you doing this?

Billy   Doing what?

Azeem   You know what!

Billy   How come you haven't got your Gunga Din costume on . . . aren't you going to the Mosque today?

Beat.

Azeem   Yeah, I am . . . in a bit . . . I'm going to put it on before I go . . . and I'm going to march right down that street.

Sheila   Good boy, Azeem.

Azeem *throws his mam a sharp look.* **Billy** *notices.*

Billy   There's a revolution going on in this house by the look of things.

Azeem   Is that what you're doing, having a revolution?

Billy   Like Ali says . . . a mental revolution.

Sheila   Your dad would have been ashamed of you.

Billy   He's not here, so it doesn't matter does it?

Sheila   You just don't care do you?

Billy   Care about what?

Sheila   What people think.

Billy   You didn't.

Sheila   If you're going to dress like that . . . there's no place for you in this house . . . you've done what you've done . . . and I'm going to give you some time to grow your hair back . . . and if you don't then I want you out . . .

Azeem   Mam . . .

Sheila   I've had enough of him.

Sheila *heads to the door.*

Billy   If you're going to the kitchen grab us some ketchup.

Sheila   Get your own bloody ketchup!

Sheila *leaves muttering . . .* **Billy** *laughs, gets up and goes and gets himself the ketchup.*

In the kitchen a discombobulated **Sheila** *tries to look busy as* **Billy** *enters, grabs the ketchup and leaves.* **Sheila** *watches him go and then bursts into tears.*

Billy   You want some?

Azeem   They're fried in animal fat . . .

Billy   Go on, have a chip . . . I dare you.

Azeem   Dare me . . . I'm not ten! Is that what you and your mates do . . . dare each other . . . go and knock on that door and we'll run away . . . I dare you . . . Mam was right . . . you're like Aunty Mary.

Billy   Is that what Mam says about me . . . no surprise there . . . go on have one of these chips . . . I'll give you a pound.

Azeem   I wouldn't eat that if you gave me a tenner.

Billy   Wouldn't you? Here . . .

Billy *goes into his pocket and pulls out a wad of money.*

Billy   Have one and I'll give you twenty quid.

Azeem   Where did you get that money?

Billy   Have a chip and I'll tell you.

Azeem   Fuck you.

Billy   Please yourself.

Azeem *stays silent.* **Billy** *savours his fish and chips. He opens the paper and reads as he eats.*

Azeem   She's going to kick you out.

Billy   So.

Azeem   So . . . so? What about us?

Billy   You two can carry on playing happy families . . . you seem to enjoy it.

Azeem   But . . .

Billy   Ali's coming . . . I told you he was going to come . . . you were both laughing at me . . . not laughing now . . . how brilliant is that . . . it's all anyone can talk about out there . . . it says here that they've got this sculptor . . . Ken Rowden . . . to make a statue of him . . . they're going to present it to him after a fancy dinner at the town hall . . . he's going to have a walk around Gypsies Green . . . obviously . . . do you know of this Ken Rowden?

Azeem   Why would I know him?

Billy   I thought that was your thing these days . . . I seen your pamphlets about art college . . . is that what you're going to do . . . go to art college . . . good for you . . . that's really going to fuck Mam off.

Azeem   Are you going to go and see him dressed like that?

Beat.

Billy   Why not?

Azeem   People are going to laugh at you.

Billy   Not to my face . . . they wouldn't dare . . .

Azeem   And that's alright with you?

Billy   People laugh at you . . . to your face . . . it doesn't seem to bother you.

Azeem   Who laughs at me?

Billy   When you've got your baggy pants on and your little hat . . . what do you think they're doing?

Azeem   I ignore them.

Billy   Well you're a better man than me.

Azeem   Too right I am!

Billy   Everybody is a hero when they're sat at home . . .

Azeem   What do you know . . . my mates have got a band . . . they got a gig . . . I'm going to see them . . .

Billy   Fuck off . . . what friends have you got?

Azeem   See . . . you think you know it all . . . but you don't know anything.

Billy   I'm talking about people that are normal.

Azeem   Is that what you are . . . normal . . . dressed like that?

Billy   More normal than you are.

Azeem   I wouldn't want to be like that . . . Mam always says . . .

Billy   Yeah Mam always says . . . that's how normal you are . . . you're such a fucking fanny . . . she's turned you into a little wuss . . . scared of your own fucking shadow!

Azeem   I'm not scared of anything . . . I'm not scared of fucking you!

Billy   You should be.

Azeem   Why . . . what you going to do . . . fuck my begonias up?

Billy *jumps up, grabs a handful of chips and forces them into* **Azeem**'*s mouth.* **Azeem** *struggles in vain as the much stronger* **Billy** *succeeds in getting them into his mouth.*

In the kitchen **Sheila** *hears the commotion, quickly composes herself and comes rushing into the living room.*

She enters as **Azeem** *is spitting out the chips.*

Sheila   What the hell's going on?

Billy   Go on tell her! . . . tell her mammy's boy! . . . go fucking crying to her!

Beat.

Azeem   Nowt! There's nowt going on! I'm going out with my mates.

Scene Seven

'White Riot' by The Clash plays.

Azeem *is nervously watching people enjoying the gig. He tries a few tentative moves. This grows as* **Azeem** *loses his inhibitions and starts to get into the music. This turns to* **Azeem** *being in his element, rocking the night away.*

Lights fade, when they come up **Azeem** *is walking home. He is full of the adrenalin of his night out. A noise makes him spin.*

Voice   What the fuck are you doing around here you Paki!

Voice   Do the black bastard!

Azeem *runs.*

We then see **Azeem***, bloodied and broken, crawl onto the stage.*

He collapses.

Billy *runs onto the stage. He looks around to make sure the others have gone. Then he lifts* **Azeem** *and carries him away.*

Scene Eight

A battered and bruised **Azeem***, he has his eyes shut.* **Sheila** *fusses around him.*

Sheila   What do you fancy eating . . . you haven't eaten properly for days . . . you'll be starving . . . I'll do you something you like . . . how about some egg and chips . . .

you love egg and chips . . . or I can do you a curry, do you fancy a curry?

Beat.

Silence from **Azeem**.

Sheila   Do you want a blanket, let me get you a blanket . . .

Sheila *grabs a blanket and puts it over* **Azeem**.

Sheila   Next week I'll nip over to your school and talk to your teachers about getting you some work to do so you don't fall behind . . . I know you're miles ahead of anyone, but you want to do well your exams don't you . . . let me know which teachers I need to speak to and I'll go over.

Azeem *opens his eyes.*

Azeem   I'm not going back.

Sheila   Don't worry we won't rush things . . . when you're right.

Azeem   I'm not going back at all.

Sheila   What do you mean?

Azeem   Which bit can't you understand . . . I'm not going back.

Sheila   Don't be daft.

Azeem   I've made up my mind.

Beat.

Sheila   Things are going to be alright . . . you're going to get past this . . . you'll move past it son . . .

Azeem   Plenty of lads leave school at fifteen.

Sheila   I know they do son . . . but look what happens to them . . . they have no life . . . no security . . . they're at the mercy of others . . .

Azeem   And I'm not . . . look at me.

Sheila   The bruises will heal son . . .

Azeem   It's not the bruises Mam . . .

Sheila   People will respect you Azeem, they'll look up to you. Don't you want that?

Azeem   Mam, they didn't ask me if I was a doctor.

Sheila   Azeem, think about what you're saying son . . . a rash decision now is going to affect the rest of your life . . . it'll ruin it . . . you've got to trust me son . . . you'll live to regret a decision like this.

Azeem   I'll be alright.

Sheila   No you won't . . . it's a hard, hard world son . . . and the choices we make follow us for the rest of our lives . . . trust me, I know . . .

Sheila *looks down at her shalwar kameez, she feels restricted by it, she starts pulling at it – from this moment until the end of the scene she starts to take it off.*

Azeem   I'm not going back . . . I've made up my mind.

Sheila   And what are you going to do?

Azeem   There are plenty of jobs . . . I'll get one. Me dad got a job . . . I will.

Beat.

Sheila   Are you some sort of idiot! Did that kick to your head give you brain damage! What are you going on about you'll get a job like your dad! Do you even know what he went through?

Azeem   He worked didn't he?

Sheila   He didn't just work . . . he toiled!

Azeem   I'll toil . . .

Sheila   It's not just a word! Do you have any idea what toiling means? Your dad got up at the break of day, in all sorts of weather and walked to those pits and those yards not even sure he'd get a day's work . . . he stood around till they'd given all the work to the white lads and then if there was any left . . . he got a shift . . . and it was always the worst . . . the jobs no else wanted to do . . .

Azeem   I'll be alright.

Sheila   No you won't! Use that massive brain of yours and think about what you're doing!

Azeem   You and Dad did alright.

Sheila   No we never! Every day was a fight! The things we went through to make sure you two were alright . . . the sacrifices we made . . . the grief we took . . . the abuse we put up with . . . for you two!

Azeem   I didn't ask you to do any of that.

Sheila   You know what you can fuck off! Do whatever you want . . . and your brother . . . and fuck that father of yours as well and his head full of dreams . . . I fell for that 'everything is going to be alright' once . . . I'm not going to again . . . I've had enough . . . I'm out of here!

Sheila *goes to her wardrobe and rifles through it – grabs a skirt and a top, throws them on and stomps out of the house.*

Scene Nine

Azeem *wakes to find the room is in darkness. He takes a moment then stands, the Muhammad Ali book he was reading falls to the floor. He switches on lights, then goes and picks up the book. He reads a paragraph.*

Azeem   *'Only a man who knows what it is like to be defeated can reach down to the bottom of his soul and come up with the extra ounce of power it takes to win.'*

He considers this a moment, then carefully marks the page and puts the book down.

He turns to an imaginary foe.

Azeem   What was that?

He listens to the imaginary answer. **Azeem** *acts out this confrontation.*

Azeem   Listen mate . . .

Azeem   I know I'm not your mate . . . I'm trying to be polite to you.

Azeem   I don't want any trouble . . . I just want to go about my business.

Azeem   Do you want to get out of my way.

Azeem   Look, I've told you, I don't want any trouble.

Azeem   Don't touch me.

Azeem   I'm warning you don't touch.

Azeem   Why? Well because . . . Bang! Bang! Bang!

Azeem *throws three punches at his imaginary foe. He quickly spins to confront the rest of them.*

Azeem   You might want to pick him up and take him to hospital . . . he's got a broken jaw.

Azeem   Well fair enough . . . if that's the way you want this to go . . . Bang! Bang! Bang!

He lays out another foe.

Azeem   You don't remember me do you . . . why would you . . . you jumped me . . . a gang of you.

Azeem *moves around the kitchen like it was a ring.*

He throws jabs, uppercuts and hooks.

Azeem   Not so fucking hard now are you? Bang! Bang! Bang!

More punches.

Azeem   You picked on the wrong man this time didn't you! Bang! Bang! Bang!

More punches, combinations, dancing around the kitchen.

Azeem   Come on, is that best you've got? Bang! Bang! Bang!

Azeem   Is that your fucking lot? Bang! Bang! Bang!

Azeem   Come on then! Let's do it! Bang! Bang! Bang!

Azeem   You're running now! Not so fast! Bang! Bang! Bang!

Billy *enters the house; he is dog tired and looks rough. He has a carrier bag containing a bulky item. He's not dressed as a skinhead anymore.*

In the kitchen **Azeem** *is unaware, he carries on his imaginary fight.*

Azeem   Not so hard now are you . . . not so hard when someone fights back! Bang! Bang! Bang!

Billy *hears* **Azeem** *and makes his way to the kitchen.* **Azeem** *has his back to him and is just finishing off the last assailant.*

Azeem   That's it, run you fuckers! Run!

Billy   Fancy some dal?

Azeem *spins around to see* **Billy** *watching him. He's mortified. He hesitates, not sure what to do.*

Azeem   Did you come to watch the Ali interview?

Billy   Is there another one on tonight?

Azeem   Yeah . . . there's been loads of stuff on.

Billy   Is Mam going to let you watch it?

Azeem   I don't care.

Billy   Where has she gone?

Azeem   Out.

Billy   Did she go and see The Queen?

Azeem   Did you?

Billy   I was out and about but I didn't join in.

Azeem   What was it like?

Billy   Busy . . . loads going on . . . street parties, flag waving
. . . everything you'd expect . . . how come Mam never went?

Azeem   She was in here with me all day . . . then she was
raging and she left.

Billy   Why?

Azeem   Because I told her I'm wrapping in school.

Billy   What are you doing that for you idiot?

Beat.

Billy   Why do you want to wrap in school?

Azeem   I got jumped . . .

Billy   So you want to pack in because of that.

Azeem   Where the fuck were you?

Beat.

Billy   Are you just going to let them win?

Azeem   They kicked fuck out of me!

Billy   I can see . . .

He adds a splash of water.

Azeem   You'll know who they are won't you?

Billy   *Silence.*

Azeem   I want to fight them . . . one on one.

Billy   What good's that going to do you?

Azeem   I want to kick their fucking heads in!

Billy   I didn't ask that . . . I asked what good it's going to do you.

Azeem   It's going to give me satisfaction.

Billy   Don't you think you'd get more satisfaction when they come into your doctor's surgery with the clap and you give them the wrong medicine or something like that.

Azeem   I can't wait that long.

Billy   Why not?

Azeem   Because it's killing me . . . I feel humiliated . . . it's all I can think about. Are you going to find out who these lads are?

Billy   Don't worry, you'll get your revenge.

Azeem   When?

Billy   When you've sat your exams.

Azeem   I told you . . . I'm not going back! I'm going to fight them!

Billy   You couldn't fight sleep . . . don't you think you should learn how to fight before you go looking for them . . .

Azeem   But . . .

Billy   You go unprepared and you're likely to get beat up again . . . come on, this interview will be on . . . bring that bag.

Azeem *grabs the bag and they go and sit in front of the TV. Their programme hasn't started yet.*

Azeem   What's this?

Billy   I go you something . . . go on then.

He takes the bag and unwraps it. He reveals a Muhammad Ali statue.

Azeem   Whoa! Where did you get this?

Billy   I seen it and thought you'd like it.

Azeem   That's beautiful . . . why did you get me it?

Billy   'Thanks Billy, that's brilliant.'

Azeem   Thanks Billy.

Azeem *admires the trophy.*

Billy   Don't wrap school in . . . it'll fuck your life up.

Azeem   My life's already fucked.

Billy   Shut up you dickhead! You're fucking fifteen! You haven't got a life.

Azeem *has a moment of realisation.*

Azeem   Hang around . . . this sculpture is that sculpture isn't it?

Billy   It's your sculpture now.

Azeem   What the fuck are you doing!

Billy   It's only a sculpture.

Azeem   It's Muhammad Ali's sculpture!

Billy   No . . . it isn't his till they give it to him . . . it's the council's sculpture.

Azeem   You'll get locked up.

Billy *shrugs this off.*

Azeem   You've got to give it back.

Billy   Don't you want it?

Beat.

Azeem   Why did you throw that bleach over the fella's flowers?

Beat.

Billy   Doesn't matter about that.

Azeem   Go on, tell me.

Billy   It doesn't make any difference now.

Azeem   It does . . . I want to know.

Beat.

Billy   I was going out with a girl . . . Lisa . . . she was gorgeous.

Azeem   Did she have really long ginger hair?

Billy   Yeah, how do you know?

Azeem   Me, Mam and Dad seen you once . . . in town . . . you were talking to this girl . . . with really long hair . . . she was beautiful . . . and you can tell you weren't just talking to her . . . you know what I mean.

Billy   I do.

Azeem   Mam wanted to come over and say hello . . . but Dad said that we should leave you be . . . said we shouldn't cramp your style.

Billy   Did he?

Beat.

Azeem   Yeah, so what happened?

Billy   So one day I'm around at hers . . . this posh house, got a garden and all sorts . . . and her dad . . . he's this big fella . . . and I mean massive . . . and he starts saying all these racist things . . . Black bastard this and Paki that . . .

Azeem   About you?

Billy   No . . . he thought I was a white lad . . . he was saying them . . . and they were all laughing . . . and you could tell this was regular craic . . .

Azeem   Didn't this Lisa tell him?

Billy   She didn't know.

Azeem   Didn't you tell her?

Billy   I was scared.

Beat.

Billy   So he starts saying all these racist things and I had to sit there and listen . . . and pretend . . . pretend that I was okay with what he was saying . . .

Azeem   Were you?

Billy   Of course I wasn't, you dickhead!

Beat.

Sorry . . . so I listened, kept my mouth shut . . . he was massive . . . there was nowt I could have done to him . . . anyway . . . that night I went back and threw bleach all over his flowers . . . he loved those fucking flowers.

Azeem   How did you get caught?

Billy   The neighbour over the road is only one of those curtain-twitcher types . . . you know, nosy cow . . . she spots me and phones the coppers . . . there must have been a patrol round and about . . . I wasn't there for more than ten minutes . . . next thing you know . . . this fucking police car comes screeching up.

Azeem   Didn't you run?

Billy   Yeah but they caught me . . . got locked up . . . charged me with criminal damage . . . got myself a criminal record . . . mad how one choice can change the course of your life.

Beat.

Azeem   So what happened?

Billy   What do you mean, 'what happened?'

Azeem   You went from throwing bleach over some fella's flowers for being a racist to being a skinhead . . . what happened?

Billy   I don't know.

Azeem   Something must have happened.

Billy   I remember this like it was yesterday . . . I was only a
nipper . . . I was in the park with Dad . . . and I'm on the
swings . . . and this fella walks over with his kid . . . about the
same age as Dad, the kid's a bit younger than me . . . I can
still see him now . . . and there's empty swings . . . but he
starts saying that I should get off the swing so his son can use
it and Dad looks at the other swings . . . you know the free
ones . . . he doesn't say anything, just looks at the swings . . .
then this fella just spits in Dad's face . . . just like that . . . he
spits in Dad's face . . . and Dad doesn't do anything . . . he
says 'come on Bilal, we're going' . . . and me and Dad walk
home . . . don't say a word to each other.

Azeem   Did you tell Mam?

Billy   No . . . but the night he died . . . we were arguing . . .
it started with the usual stuff about getting a job, living a
respectable life and all that . . . it got a bit tasty and he's
going on about turning the other cheek and keeping your
head down . . . and I told him . . . I reminded him of that
day . . . and . . . and . . . you know . . . said some horrible
things . . . the last thing I ever said to him was that I thought
he was a coward . . . I didn't know did I . . . I didn't know
that I'd never speak to him again . . .

Azeem   Fuck.

Billy   Yeah . . . fuck . . . I didn't want it to be like that . . .
and the only thing I thought of was . . . this is going to sound
mad . . . but . . . if you can't beat them . . . join them . . .

Azeem   And?

Billy   I found out . . . the hard way . . . that they're more
lost than I am.

*We hear the interviewer theme tune. The boys turn their attention
towards the TV.*

Azeem *watches his brother.*

Azeem   How did you find out?

Billy   Let's watch this . . . it's brilliant.

Azeem   How did you find out?

Billy   Shush! It's about to start.

Scene Ten

Sheila *is in a pub, it's a lively night.*

She is apprehensive at first, she nervously sips at her drink.

In the background we can hear singing, some people joining in.

Sheila *smiles at a few people, gives others a little wave.*

She starts to get into it.

The singing stops, now there is just the sound of the drinkers in the pub.

Sheila *downs her drink, takes a deep breath and heads to the mic and picks it up.*

She starts to sing.

Sheila
> *My young love said to me.*
> *My mother won't mind.*

The noise in the pub abates.

Sheila
> *And my father won't slight you.*
> *For your lack of kine.*
> *And she stepped away from me.*
> *And this she did say:*
> *It will not be long, love.*
> *Till our wedding day.*

The pub falls silent.

She stepped away from me.
And she moved through the fair.
And fondly I watched her.
Move here and there.
And then she went homeward.
With one star awake.
Like the swan in the evening.
Moves over . . .

We hear the doors open. **Sheila** *abruptly stops singing, but she is disappointed.*

Sheila   Sorry folks . . . I was hoping my sisters were going to be in here tonight . . . you'll know them, Mary and Siobhan O'Doherty . . . Mary goes by Kelly now . . . Mary Kelly . . . Siobhan is a Peters.

Beat.

Sheila   I've been thinking a lot about them a lot this last twelve months . . . how life's treating them? I've got to admit, I've had a rocky twelve months . . . my husband died . . . I miss him . . . I wanted to tell my sisters . . . you know, that he's gone . . . tell them myself you know . . . I'm sure they've heard from others . . . but we don't talk . . . they haven't talked to me for the best part of twenty years.

Beat.

Sheila   I think it's important that they hear it from me . . . when our dad died . . . they got a message to me to say that I wasn't welcome at the funeral . . . when my mam died . . . they sent another message . . . I wasn't planning on going anyway . . . they don't talk to me because I married a Pakistani man.

Beat.

Sheila   They made me choose, it's us or him . . . I chose him . . . they said 'he's not one of us'.

She looks around the room with disdain.

Sheila   Shall I tell you what, my Sadiq was one of us . . . he was one of those that aren't welcome . . . he laughed like us, he loved like us, he cried like us and . . . he bled like us . . . and he died like us . . . from a heart attack . . . like me dad . . . Remember those signs those signs that said No Irish, No Blacks, No Dogs . . .

Beat.

Sheila   But of course you remember . . . some of you had those signs in your windows and now you don't put them in your window, you keep them in your head.

Sheila looks at the drinkers with disdain.

I'll be seeing you.

She leaves.

Sheila *walks home.*

We hear **Lag ja Gale***.*

Sheila *looks around . . . where is the music coming from?*

She smiles at a memory.

Sheila   Remember the night you explained the words to me Sadiq? . . . 'take me in your arms – we don't know whether we'll ever have another night like this again'. I miss you my love.

Scene Eleven

We return to the boys, they are in full flow as Ali and the interviewer.

We return to the pastiche – Ali is seething when interviewers refer to contradictions in Ali's beliefs and views on white American society. The boys have just seen the segment where Ali feels that the interviewer has tried to trap him on live TV to make him look bad. Ali proclaims that the interviewer does not have the mental depth or agility to corner Ali on TV and challenges him to ask any question he

*likes, and Ali will destroy his points right there on national
television.*

Azeem *can't take his eyes off* **Billy**. **Billy** *can't look* **Azeem** *in the
eye. He looks at the TV intensely instead.*

Azeem   They arrested one of the lads that jumped me.

Billy   Did they . . . has he said owt?

Azeem   What would he say?

Billy   Who his mates were.

Azeem   I don't know . . . haven't you heard owt?

Beat.

Billy   The thing with this interview is that the interviewer
thinks he's cleverer than Ali . . . but he isn't.

Azeem   He's a very clever man . . . sharp . . . works things
out.

Billy   He thinks that because Ali's a boxer he can trap him.

Azeem   But he can't because Ali's sussed him out . . . so
where were you?

Billy   When?

Azeem   When I got jumped.

Billy   I was in Toon.

Azeem   How did you hear about me getting jumped?

Billy   Did you see that . . . did you see how he ripped him
to shreds . . . on the telly in front of the whole country . . . he
makes him look like a fucking chump!

Azeem   How did you know?

Billy   Because I've seen it before.

Azeem   Not that . . . how did you know about me getting
jumped?

Billy   Did you see what Ali has just done to that interviewer . . . didn't you see that . . . he tried trapping him but Ali was too clever for him . . . Ali told him the truth!

Azeem   You were there weren't you?

Billy   Ali takes no prisoners! What needs to be done . . . needs to be done!

Azeem   You were my brother.

Billy   And he's coming here tomorrow! To see us . . . to be with us!

Azeem   What did I ever do to you?

Billy   And they're all going to be cheering him. He's going to be visiting the boys' clubs . . . he's going to Gypsies Green for a walk about . . . then they're going to go to the Mosque, to get his wedding blessed . . . you should be there . . . you should go . . . He's staying for four days you know . . . Muhammad Ali in South Shields for four whole days . . .

Azeem   You were supposed to look after me.

Billy   And who the fuck is looking after me, eh!

Silence.

Don't I deserve to be looked after . . . don't I deserve to be respected . . . don't I deserve to loved! Go on . . . tell me . . . tell me who loves me!

Azeem   I love you.

Billy   You've got a funny way of showing it!

Azeem   And how did you show it . . . by kicking me . . . by turning your back on me when I needed you the most.

Billy   What about when I was getting kicked!

Sheila *enters and listens.*

Azeem   Who was kicking you?

Billy   The whole fucking world! Didn't you ever think . . .
didn't you ever think what it was like for me.

Azeem   You had everything.

Billy   I had white skin and a brown name.

Azeem   I've got brown skin and a brown name.

Billy   At least you know who you are.

Azeem   But they can't accept who I am.

Billy   They don't accept who I am.

Azeem   Why?

Billy   Because we're not the same.

Azeem   We are the same! We hurt and we bleed and we cry
just like any other fucker!

Billy   They don't care.

Azeem   They've got to care . . . someone's got to fucking
care!

Billy   No they don't . . . they're never going to accept us.

Sheila *enters.*

Sheila   Fuck them!

We've got to accept each other . . . that's all we've got . . . us
. . . just us here . . . this family . . . we can't live our lives
waiting for them to give us something . . . to recognise us . . .
to have love or have compassion for us . . . they're full of
fucking hate! Remember what I'm telling you . . . don't rely
on them . . . they'll break your hearts and fill you with rage
. . . and they're not worth that . . . we're going to have find
what we need in each other . . . that's what your dad would
have told you . . .

Billy   But he isn't here is he . . . he's had it away on his
toes . . .

Azeem   Shut the fuck up! Don't say that . . . don't say that about him!

Billy   I want my fucking dad!

Azeem   I want him to be in that kitchen listening to his music, cooking us food . . . why can't I have that?

Sheila *enters.*

Sheila   Because he's gone, son . . . he's gone and we have to pick up the pieces of what's left.

Billy *bursts into tears, broken.*

Billy   What are we going to do, Mam?

Sheila *takes her son in her arms.*

Azeem *sits and cries.*

Billy *clings to his mam, inbetween racking sobs he keeps asking . . .*

Billy   What are we going to do?

Eventually **Sheila** *takes her son's face in her hands.*

Sheila   We're going to fight, Bilal . . . we're going to fight and we're going to carry on fighting, son . . . 'you don't lose when you get knocked down . . . you lose when you fail to get back up'.

She turns to **Azeem** *and beckons him over.*

The three hug.

Scene Twelve

The two brothers are having a boxing pads session.

They move around the ring like a dance.

Billy *wears the pads.*

Azeem *wears the gloves.*

They deliver the lines alternately: a duet.

Billy   Name?

Azeem   Muhammad Ali . . . The 'Louisville Lip'.

Billy   Born?

Azeem   Cassius Marcellus Clay.

Billy   On?

Azeem   17 January 1942.

Billy   He started boxing at?

Azeem   Twelve.

Billy   Kentucky Golden Gloves titles?

Azeem   Six.

Billy   National Golden Gloves titles?

Azeem   Two.

Billy   Became Olympic Champion at?

Azeem   Eighteen.

Billy   At?

Azeem   1960 Rome Olympics.

Billy   Champion of the world at?

Azeem   Twenty-two.

Billy   He beat?

Azeem   Sonny Liston to became the youngest heavyweight champion ever.

Billy   Good lad.

Azeem   The next day . . . He declared he was a Muslim.

Billy   And his name was now?

Azeem   Muhammad Ali.

Billy   What did he say?

Azeem   'I don't want no slave name.'

Billy   What happened in the Ernie Terrell fight?

Azeem   Terrell wouldn't call him Muhammad Ali . . . He kept calling him Cassius Clay.

Billy   What did Ali do?

Azeem   He battered him for fifteen rounds.

Billy   All the time asking him?

Azeem *hits the pads with each word: 'What's. My. Name!'*

Azeem   When they tried to send him to Vietnam he said?

Billy   'I ain't got no quarrel with them Viet-Cong.' And refused to go . . . what did they do?

Azeem   They banned him from boxing. Took his titles away. And tried sending him to prison.

Billy   How long was he out of the ring?

Azeem   Three years . . . During his prime.

Billy   When he fought Ken Norton, he boxed with a broken jaw for ten rounds.

Azeem   He fought Joe Frazier three times.

Billy   Winning twice.

Azeem   These fights are considered some of the greatest fights of all time.

Billy   He fought George Foreman.

Azeem   'The Rumble in the Jungle.'

Billy   What round did stop him on?

Azeem   The eighth round.

Billy   Becoming the first man in boxing history to win the heavyweight title three times.

Azeem   He wasn't just a supreme athlete . . .

Billy   He was an entertainer.

Azeem   A raconteur.

Billy   You and your long words! He was poet.

Azeem   An activist.

Billy   A thinker.

Azeem   A humanist.

Billy   A revolutionary!

Azeem   He did it all with style.

Billy   And skill.

Azeem   And beauty.

Billy   And grace!

Azeem   'Float like a butterfly –

Billy   – Sting like a bee.'

The boys raise their arms . . . Ali style.

Billy/Azeem   And he came to South Shields.

Scene Thirteen

The boys are making their way to the Muhammad Ali procession.
Azeem *has his camera. They laugh and joke.*

Billy *gets* **Azeem** *in a headlock. Excited!*

Billy   Muhammad Ali's here kid! Can you believe that!

Azeem   Get off me you dickhead!

Azeem *gives* **Billy** *a sneaky kidney punch to get free of him.*

Billy   We'll head over to Gypsies Green after this . . . he's going to take on the darts champion.

Azeem   Darts?

Billy   For a laugh . . . have you got your ticket for the Mosque . . . don't be losing that.

Azeem   I've got it safe at home . . . sorry I couldn't get you one.

Billy   Don't worry about it . . . he's coming to the gym . . . I might get a chance to spar with him . . . I could be sparring with Muhammad Ali . . . wouldn't that be the business.

Billy *rubs his side where* **Azeem** *punched him.*

Billy   It fucking hurt that!

Azeem   Yeah, don't work your ticket or you'll be getting spark'oed.

Billy   Dickhead!

Billy *looks over his shoulder expectantly.* **Azeem** *follows suit.*

They are disappointed

They reach their spot on the route. They take in the crowds.

Billy   Can you believe how many people have turned out . . . I knew there were going to be loads . . . but not this many.

Azeem   He's using the same open-top bus as The Queen.

Billy   Because he's the KING!

Azeem   There's a parade of Champions happening as well.

Billy   Aye, John Conteh is coming up . . . some other professional boxers . . . there's some exhibition bouts over at Washington.

Azeem   Aya going?

Billy   Going to try and get some tickets . . . we'll both go.

Azeem   He's doing this thing in Newcastle as well.

Billy   They always try and get in on the act them lot . . . aww mate this is class!

The boys wait expectantly when after a moment **Sheila** *pushes her way through to them,*

Sheila   What a nightmare that was . . . trying to get through that crowd . . . this is what it would be like if the Toon ever won a trophy.

Billy   Fat chance of that.

Azeem   Are they rubbish?

Sheila *and* **Billy** *share a look.*

Sheila *takes in the crowd. She notices something.*

Sheila   He's risking his child allowance, that one, isn't he?

The boys look around.

Sheila   That one there, sat up on that road sign . . . like razor blades them things.

Billy   It's worth it.

Sheila   Shut up you silly sod.

They laugh.

Azeem   I read that when he's doing roadwork, he wears heavy boots so that when he puts his boxing boots on, they're light as a feather.

Beat.

Billy   Remember that time Dad glued the soles of his boots back on . . .

They laugh.

Sheila   I told the silly bugger the glue wasn't dry yet.

Billy   I've got them on!

More laughter.

Billy   The glue seeped through, and he managed to glue his feet to the boots.

More laughter.

Azeem   You told him to wear a pair of socks before trying them on.

More laughter.

Sheila   Nobody listens to what I say in that house.

We hear a gentle roar.

Billy   Can you hear that . . . he's coming.

The roar grows louder. **Azeem** *readies his camera.*

Billy   Leave that! . . . Enjoy the moment!

The roar grows louder.

Azeem   I will . . . I will . . . promise . . . but let me get a couple for the memory.

Billy   Get one of me with him in the background.

He poses for a photograph arms raised like Ali, but then grabs his mum and they both pose for the photograph.

Azeem   Say . . .

He thinks a moment.

Azeem   'What's my name?'

Billy/Sheila   What's my name!

The roar is deafening,

People are chanting 'ALI! ALI! ALI!'.

Azeem *takes his photos, then stops.*

They are all looking up towards an open-top bus.

They look with admiration and awe as the bus slowly inches past them until it has gone.

Lights fade.

The end.